The Call with Promise:

How to Receive the Best from God

by Richmond Donkor

Copyright © 2016 by Richmond Donkor
All rights reserved. No part of this book may be reproduced, stored in a retrieval system, or transmitted in any form or by any means, electronic, mechanical, photocopying, recording, scanning, or otherwise, without the prior written permission of the publisher.

Edited by Adam M. Swiger (www.lifesgiftsllc.com)

Scripture references are taken from the following versions (all emphasis in text added unless otherwise noted):

Scripture quotations marked (CEB) are taken from the Common English Bible®, CEB® Copyright © 2010, 2011 by Common English Bible.™ Used by permission. All rights reserved worldwide. The "CEB" and "Common English Bible" trademarks are registered in the United States Patent and Trademark Office by Common English Bible. Use of either trademark requires the permission of Common English Bible.
Scripture quotations marked (ESV) are taken from The ESV® Bible (The Holy Bible, English Standard Version®) copyright © 2001 by Crossway, a publishing ministry of Good News Publishers. ESV® Text Edition: 2011. The ESV® text has been reproduced in cooperation with and by permission of Good News Publishers. Unauthorized reproduction of this publication is prohibited. Used by permission. All rights reserved.

Scripture quotations marked (KJV) are taken from the King James Bible. Accessed on Bible Gateway. www.BibleGateway.com.

Scripture marked (MSG) are taken from The Message. Copyright © 1993, 1994, 1995, 1996, 2000, 2001, 2002. Used by permission of NavPress Publishing Group.
Scripture quotations marked (NASB) are taken from the New American Standard Bible ® (NASB), copyright © 1960, 1962, 1963, 1968, 1971, 1972, 1973, 1975, 1977, 1995 by The Lockman Foundation. Used by permission. www.Lockman.org.
Scripture quotations marked (NIV) are taken from the Holy Bible, New International Version. Copyright © 1973, 1978, 1984, 2011 by Biblica, Inc.® Used by permission. All rights reserved worldwide.

Scripture quotations marked (NKJV) are taken from the New King James Version®. Copyright © 1982 by Thomas Nelson, Inc. Used by permission. All rights reserved.
Scripture quotations marked (NLT) are taken from the Holy Bible, New Living Translation, copyright © 1996, 2004, 2007 by Tyndale House Foundation. Used by permission of Tyndale House Publishers, Inc., Carol Stream, Illinois 60188. All rights reserved.

Cover design, internal formatting & layout by Hemant Lal
www.AaronProductionsIndia.com

Now if you belong to Christ, then indeed you are Abraham's descendants, heirs according to the promise.

(Galatians 3:29 CEB)

Table of Contents

Introduction 7

Chapter One: Abraham's Family 17

Chapter Two: The Calling Stage 23

Chapter Three: Three Requirements of the Calling 33

Chapter Four: The Promise Stage 41

Chapter Five: The Law of Believing 54

Chapter Six: The Expalanation of the Law of Believing . . . 63

Chapter Seven: The Success Stage 74

Chapter Eight: One Step at a Time 84

Chapter Nine: Abraham the Forgiver 104

Chapter Ten: Abraham the Giver 117

Chapter Eleven: Why Tithes and Offering 130

Chapter Twelve: Abraham the Just 140

Chapter Thirteen: Abraham the Believer 149

Chapter Fourteen: Abraham's Trials and Blessings 164

Chapter Fifteen: The Principle of Accountability 189

Chapter Sixteen: Accountability Questions 202

Conclusion 207

INTRODUCTION

In daily life, people always call you with a purpose. Anytime someone calls you, either the person informs you of his or her reason for calling or you end up asking why the person called.

This is similar to the call of God. He calls us from the kingdom of darkness to the kingdom of light, and each and every one of us—like Abraham, patriarch of the Israelites—has something to accomplish for His glory. Some of us still don't know the purpose of our calling, and perhaps we have given up our dreams and goals in life. When God called Abraham, however, He gave him some promises; and all of those promises came to pass. God has attached certain promises to your calling as well—and it is time for you to discover what they are.

Negative and discouraging words from friends and relatives sometimes make us feel that we are not important in life. Perhaps you have never heard anyone say a single positive thing about you. Even so, God is our heavenly Father, and He knows us far better than does anyone else around us. God called us for a purpose, and I believe that each and every one of us can accomplish that purpose before we leave this earth. God chose or called us from the multitude just as He called Abraham from among his people.

The way in which Abraham became an extremely successful man is a great lesson—one that every believer should know. The Bible says in Galatians 3:29, "Now if you belong to Christ, then indeed you are Abraham's descendants, heirs according to the promise" (CEB). He was seventy-five years old, and his wife sixty-five, when God told him to leave his country, his people, and his household. Today they would already have been at retirement age, when many people have given up on life or new opportunities because of their age, health, or some other excuse. Abraham did not inherit anything from his parents; but despite starting with a zero balance at the age of seventy-five, he went on to acquire massive wealth. I strongly believe that the truth contained in these pages will help every person to put his or her life priorities in the right place.

Sometimes the problems we experience in life make us feel that we have no purpose on this earth. However, allow me to draw your attention to the following fundamental principles from the book of Genesis: God has a plan for us, and He wants the best for us.

With everything that God created in Genesis 1, He had only to speak or command its existence, and it came to be. Compare Genesis 1:3–24 to Genesis 1:26, though, and notice that God did not command a human being to be formed. Humans were the culmination of creation—an end, not the means to an end.

God planned thoroughly before He created mankind. This was not unlike when parents are expecting their first child. There is great excitement over the arrival of the newborn. Parents will do everything they know to do in order to prepare for the coming baby. Just as expectant parents plan for that baby's arrival, God planned for the arrival of mankind.

After that, He gave humans everything necessary to take care of His other creations. As Genesis 1:26 recounts, "Then God said, 'Let us make mankind in our image, after our likeness. And let them have dominion over the fish of the sea and over the birds of the heavens and over all the earth and over every creeping thing that creeps on the earth'" (ESV).

In Genesis 1:27–28, God created humans in His own image and placed mankind in charge of everything else that He had created:

God created man in his own image,
in the image of God he created him;
male and female he created them.
28 And God blessed them. And God said to them, "Be fruitful and multiply and fill the earth and subdue it, and have dominion over the fish of the sea and over the birds of the heavens and over every living thing that moves on the earth." (ESV)

The book of Psalms confirms how much God loves the men and women He created:

What is man that you are mindful of him, and the son of man that you care for him? 5 Yet you have made him a little lower than the heavenly beings [angels] and crowned him with glory and honor. 6 You have given him dominion over the works of your hands; you have put all things under his feet, 7 all sheep and oxen, and also the beasts of the field, 8 the birds of the heavens, and the fish in the sea, whatever passes along the paths of the seas. (Psalm 8:4–8 ESV)

In these verses, we see beyond a doubt that God has cared deeply about humanity from the beginning. Not only did He create us specially to reflect Him but He also provided us with the entirety of His creation so that we could live healthy, happy, fulfilled lives.

I am often asked, "Why is it that some people are extremely rich while others are poor?" The simple answer to this question is: "It is a choice." By this answer, I don't mean that people choose to be poor. Rather, most people make choices in life that lead either to wealth or to poverty—materially and spiritually.

I have visited many different churches in many foreign countries where I have witnessed extreme poverty among Christians. Is that poverty the direct result of our teaching, or do people fail to apply what they learn from their preachers and teachers?

Jesus said in John 10:10, "The thief comes only to steal and kill and destroy; I have come that they may have life, and have it to the full" (NIV). A number of religious groups teach about contentment and self-sufficiency, which is not bad in and of itself. However, Deuteronomy 30:9 promises, "The LORD your God will then make you successful in everything you do. He will give you many children and numerous livestock, and he will cause your fields to produce abundant harvests, for the LORD will again delight in being good to you as he was to your ancestors" (NLT).

This verse mentions several important phrases for consideration, which signify different types of wealth and success:

- "successful in everything you do"
- "many children"
- "numerous livestock"
- "fields to produce abundant harvests"

Oftentimes, Christians and other readers focus on only one aspect of Deuteronomy 30:9—the promise of numerous children. What about being "successful in everything you do"? What about "numerous livestock," which represent the food and shelter necessary for those children and future generations?

Pastors are doing well in preaching and teaching about the salvation of souls, which is of course essential. However, teaching about salvation alone is not enough because man needs to enjoy God's blessing while on earth as well.

The Bible says that every human being consists of body, spirit, and soul. Genesis 2:7 recounts that "then the LORD God formed the man of dust [body] from the ground and breathed [spirit] into his nostrils the breath of life, and the man became a living creature [soul]" (ESV). Paul also said in 1 Thessalonians 5:23, "Now, may the God of peace himself cause you to be completely dedicated to him; and may your spirit, soul, and body be kept intact and blameless at our Lord Jesus Christs's coming" (CEB).

These three components of every person—body, soul, and spirit—must be fed with physical food, with the Word of God, and with friendship, respectively. For us to take proper care of the body, soul, and spirit, we must live a life with a purpose. If someone asks you what your purpose in life is, what will you tell him or her? God planned perfectly for us before He created us.

According to Genesis 1:29–30, God gave mankind green plants to feed their physical bodies:

Then God said, "Behold, I have given you every plant yielding seed that is on the surface of all the earth, and every tree which has fruit yielding seed; it shall be food for you; 30 and to every beast of the earth and to every bird of the sky and to every thing that moves on the earth which has life, I have given every green plant for food"; and it was so. (NASB)

In turn, the Bible relates, God gave mankind friendship as emotional food for the soul. Genesis 2:18 says, "Then the LORD God said, 'It is not good for the man to be alone; I will make him a helper suitable for him'" (NASB). Genesis 2:21–23 continues:

So the LORD God caused a deep sleep to fall upon the man, and he slept; then He took one of his ribs and closed up the flesh at that place. 22 The LORD God fashioned into a woman the rib which He had taken from the man, and brought her to the man. 23 The man said,

"This is now bone of my bones
And flesh of my flesh;
She shall be called Woman,
Because she was taken out of Man." (NASB)

Genesis 2:18 uses the word "helper," which means "companion" and signifies friendship. Every person's soul needs relationships in order to overcome loneliness. Because the human soul needs emotional food, people require fellowship and friendship. It is not good for man's soul to be alone.

We develop social networks as a way to provide sustenance for our souls. Such networks, whether based on personal, face-t0–face interactions or online connections, consist of souls. In the course of our interactions with others, our souls may experience excitement, irritation, or any number of other emotional reactions. Even if you have never met someone in person, you may feel comfortable and happy when you talk with him or her.

People who are unsociable or isolated, by contrast, always feel lonely within because they are not feeding the soul properly. Having a social life is not about partying, drinking, or smoking; but you need people with whom to talk, share problems, and exchange encouragement and praise. You don't need to internalize every emotion. In fact, as an old adage goes, "A problem shared is a problem half-solved."

Moreover, Ecclesiastes 4:9–12 adds:

Two are better than one, because they have a good return for their toil. 10 For if they fall, one will lift up his fellow. But woe to him who is alone when he falls and has not another to life him up! 11 Again, if two lie together, they keep warm, but how can one keep warm alone? 12 And though a man might not prevail against one who is alone, two will withstand him—a threefold cord is not quickly broken. (ESV)

Finally, as spiritual food, God has given us His Word—both written Scripture and the living Word of Jesus Christ. In Matthew 4:4 Jesus says, "It is written: 'Man shall not live on bread alone, but on every word that comes from the mouth of God'" (NIV).

Psalm 119:103, too, describes God's word as food: "How sweet are your words to my taste, sweeter than honey to my mouth!" (ESV).

Hebrews 4:12 elaborates, declaring that "God's word is living, active, and sharper than any two-edged sword. It penetrates to the point that it separates the soul from the spirit and the joints from the marrow. It's able to judge the heart's thoughts and intentions" (CEB).

For each and every person to live a balanced life, it is important to feed the body, the soul, and the spirit. A person who is hungry needs physical food in order to satisfy the hunger. Yet no physical food exists that can quench man's loneliness. Humans need other people with whom to talk or with whom to fellowship in order to overcome that loneliness. Hebrews 10:25 advises, "Don't stop meeting together with other believers, which some people have gotten into the habit of doing. Instead, encourage each other, especially as you see the day drawing near" (CEB). Even with food and fellowship, however, a person still requires spiritual food to feel complete in life.

The majority of people are not using their full potential because of their thoughts and attitudes toward life and money. The Bible did not say that money is evil; rather, the love of money is evil. Perhaps you don't love money, but you may love something else more than God. That object of love could be a problem for your spiritual wellbeing, for Jesus said, "Anyone who loves their father or mother more than me is not worthy of me; anyone who loves their son or daughter more than me is not worthy of me" (Matthew 10:37 NIV). People must choose to rely upon and follow the Word of God to live a happy and successful life.

A happy, successful life is also a useful one. The apostle Paul wrote in Ephesians 4:28, "Thieves should no longer steal. Instead, they should go to work, using their hands to do good so that they will have something to share with whoever is in need" (CEB).

It is not wrong to make money if you have the potential because money is a necessary vehicle of this life. One of the reasons why Jesus came to earth is found in 2 Corinthians 8:9, which says, "You know the grace of our Lord Jesus Christ.

Although he was rich, he became poor for our sakes, so that you could become rich through his poverty" (CEB). Learning the right way to acquire heavenly and earthly wealth is relevant to every child of God. Every person needs to set proper priorities in life. If a person's priorities are correct, he or she will make the right choices in matters great and small. However, if a person's priorities are confused, he or she will eventually fall into dark places.

Jesus came to the earth so that we would enjoy full lives while the Devil came to steal, kill, and destroy (John 10:10). Too many God-fearing people focus so intently on destroying the work of the Devil that they neglect to develop positive goals for their lives. If you are only playing defense without ever pushing forward in life, how will you gain any ground for the kingdom of God?

As we busy ourselves working for money, we should think to feed our spirit with the Word of God as well, remembering Matthew 4:4. We must also consider our human relationships because they are the food for our souls. If you isolate yourself from people because you don't trust anyone, you are denying your soul the earthly happiness that God intends.

Every person has choices to make in life, and the choices that a person makes today will determine his or her future. Most bad things that happen in a person's life are not caused by the enemy—certainly not by the Devil alone. To the contrary, most evil enters a person's life due to his or her own choices.

Most people spend more time blaming and criticizing each other—or themselves—than planning and implementing the positive truths that they have learned. The apostle Paul said in Philippians 4:8, "Finally, brothers, whatever is true, whatever is honorable, whatever is just, whatever is pure, whatever is lovely, whatever is commendable, if there is any excellence, if there is anything worthy of praise, think about these things" (ESV). We face many choices in life, so focusing on the right choices is crucial.

When it comes to acquiring spiritual and physical wealth, the story of Abraham offers us full assurance that our age and our present situation are never an excuse not to succeed. When God called you, He deposited tremendous resources and a mighty promise in you, which requires your cooperation to bring to full fruition.

CHAPTER ONE
ABRAHAM'S FAMILY

*Y*ou may well have heard the story of Abraham many times; but even so, perhaps you have not understood the practical principles that led this man to become the materially and spiritually richest man on earth. Let us, therefore, approach the story of Abraham in accordance with Psalm 90:12, which says, "So teach us to number our days, that we may apply our hearts unto wisdom" (KJV). In other words, we ought to realize how few our days truly are and, therefore, look to God's teaching to help us spend them wisely.

The most beautiful aspect of Abraham's life is how he maintained his wealth and his relationship with God. The book of Genesis reveals much about how he accomplished this—the secret behind his success.

I know that parts of the Bible can be difficult to approach or to understand, and I also recognize that the majority of people view the Bible as a book only for Christians. However, that perception couldn't be further from the truth. The Bible is a manual for every human being, no matter what he or she believes. As 2 Timothy 3:16 affirms, "Every scripture is inspired by God and is useful for teaching, for showing mistakes, for correcting, and for training character" (CEB).

In fact, the proper understanding of the Bible can be found in a mnemonic of the word "BIBLE": Basic Instructional Book for Living Every Day. The prophet Jeremiah said in Jeremiah 15:16, "Your words were found, and I ate them, and your words became to me a joy and the delight of my heart, for I am called by your name, O LORD, God of hosts" (ESV). Job also testifies that the Word of God is his daily bread, saying, "I have not departed from the commandment of his lips; I have treasured the words of his mouth more than my portion of food" (Job 23:12 ESV).

I also love the imagery in Ezekiel 3:3: "And he said to me, 'Son of man, feed your belly with this scroll that I give you and fill your stomach with it.' Then I ate it, and it was in my mouth as sweet as honey" (ESV). This book you are reading now is based on biblical principle, which will guide you step-by-step on how to create a life of wealth and fulfillment—even if you are starting from scratch.

Since every word counts, take your time and be sure to read thoroughly the Bible verses and passages presented along with the practical applications. Only by reading the scriptures will you gain a full understanding of this wealthy man named Abraham.

At the time of writing, I have spent much of the past three months watching and reading biographies of people from throughout history, up to the present day, who have tasted success. Most of these people started out poor; but because of their hard work and dedication, they became successful.

One night I attended a prayer meeting. While we were praying, the Lord told me that Abraham was a rich man—the wealthiest, in many ways—so if I wanted to know more about successful people, I should consider Abraham. I opened my eyes; and when I saw that everybody was finished praying, I grabbed my Bible and began to read the book of Genesis. When I closed my eyes again, God showed me all of the secrets to success that I now want to share with you.

Many of us have family members and acquaintances, and even close friends, who complain daily about life and the world around us. To them, it seems that life is not fair because the majority of people are suffering. However, while we do not choose to suffer, most people experience suffering because they do not understand and live by the underlying truths of life.

Genesis 11:26–31 tells us about Abraham—who lived the first part of his life as "Abram"—and his family. Understanding his family background is crucial in order to relate his starting circumstances to his later success and to our lives in the present. This is how Abraham's life began:

> After Terah had lived 70 years, he became the father of Abram, Nahor and Haran.
> 27 This is the account of Terah's family line. Terah became the father of Abram, Nahor and Haran. And Haran became the father of Lot. 28 While his father Terah was still alive, Haran died in Ur of the Chaldeans, in the land of his birth. 29 Abram and Nahor both married. The name of Abram's wife was Sarai, and the name of Nahor's wife was Milkah; she was the daughter of Haran, the father of both Milkah

and Iskah. 30 Now Sarai was childless because she was not able to conceive.

31 Terah took his son Abram, his grandson Lot son of Haran, and his daughter-in-law Sarai, the wife of his son Abram, and together they set out from Ur of the Chaldeans to go to Canaan. But when they came to Harran, they settled there. (Genesis 11:26–31 NIV)

Abraham's father was seventy years old before he had any children. These verses also suggest that the family was close-knit, dwelling and moving together. Because Abraham was the eldest son, he was supposed to inherit his father's wealth upon Terah's death. However, despite being married and advanced in years, Abraham himself had no children.

Research shows that Ur of the Chaldeans was located in the southeast corner of modern-day Iraq, some seventy-five miles north of the Kuwaiti border—right in the middle of the area where the 1991 Gulf War was fought. In Abraham's day, Ur was located at the place where the Euphrates River emptied into the Persian Gulf. At that time, trade with India and Africa was conducted at this busy seaport. According to history, not only was this city a center of commerce, but it was also a hub of scholarly activity. In fact, a large public library has been unearthed that contained thousands of ancient texts written in clay. That region was also an excellent place for raising flocks and herds—as Genesis 13:2 suggests when it says that, later on, "Abram had become very wealthy in livestock and in silver and gold" (NIV).

However, the people of Ur were involved in some of the most despicable forms of idolatry. That city was an important center for astrology and for the worship of the stars and the moon. The book of Joshua records, "And Joshua said to all the people, 'Thus says the LORD, the God of Israel: "Long ago, your fathers lived beyond the Euphrates, Terah, the father of Abraham and of Nahor; and they served other gods"'"' (Joshua 24:2 ESV).

Genesis 31:30–34 reveals that while Abraham was able to break free from the idolatry of the land, his relatives were not so fortunate. His great-nephew Laban and his grandson Jacob's future wives, Leah and Rachel, continued to live beyond the Euphrates. Many years later, Isaiah called upon the nation of Israel to remember from where God had brought them (Isaiah 51:1). Spiritually speaking, God had called their ancestor Abraham out of the most wretched of spiritual conditions!

Perhaps your family and friends are not yet believers. Pray for them, but also thank God that you have been called out from them. You, too, were swimming in sin and doing all kinds of evil things; but God called you to a life in the light. He called upon you to make a difference wherever you go and whatever you do. Let people see Christ in you!

In Romans 9:6–18, Paul explained the power of God's call and his attendant promises:

But it's not as though God's word has failed. Not all who are descended from Israel are part of Israel. 7 Not all of Abraham's children are called Abraham's descendants, but instead your descendants will be named through Isaac. 8 That means it isn't the natural children who are God's children, but it is the children from the promise who are counted as descendants. 9 The words in the promise were: A year from now I will return, and Sarah will have a son.

10 Not only that, but also Rebekah conceived children with one man, our ancestor Isaac. 11 When they hadn't been born yet and they hadn't yet done anything good or bad, it was

THE CALL WITH PROMISE

shown that God's purpose would continue because it was based on his choice. 12 It wasn't because of what was done but because of God's call...

14 So what are we going to say? Isn't this unfair on God's part? Absolutely not! 15 He says to Moses, I'll have mercy on whomever I choose to have mercy, and I'll show compassion to whomever I choose to show compassion. 16 So then, it doesn't depend on a person's desire or effort. It depends entirely on God, who shows mercy. 17 Scripture says to Pharaoh, I have put you in this position for this very thing: so I can show my power in you and so that my name can be spread through the entire earth. 18 So then, God has mercy on whomever he wants to, but he makes resistant whomever he wants to. (CEB, emphasis in original)

In this book, I will address three stages of a successful life in detail:

1. The Calling Stage

2. The Promise Stage

3. The Success Stage

First, every person must know in which stage he or she currently is. It is then helpful to know what to do at that stage to live successfully. Let us now examine each of these stages in depth.

CHAPTER TWO
THE CALLING STAGE

The call of Abraham refers to the time when God told him to leave his country, his people, and his family (Genesis 12:1). Most of the time, preachers and teachers interpret "God's call" as referring to a call to serve in ministry. That interpretation could be accurate in some cases; but the fact is that not every person is called to be a pastor or preacher or otherwise devoted to full-time, formal Christian service.

How then can the call of Abraham be applied to anyone and everyone? The answer is to realize that Abraham himself was not called to preach on the street or in a house of worship.

Much evil was taking place in Abraham's country, but God told him to leave and assured him that He would show him where to go (Genesis 12:1). However, the prevalence of idolatry in Abraham's family was not the reason why God told him to leave; rather, in immediate terms, God called Abraham to start his own business. Abraham was well aware that most people were living in sin, but he did not set out to preach a message of salvation. In fact, he was often afraid of those who lived apart from God—reasoning, for instance, "There is surely no fear of God in this place, and they will kill me because of my wife" (Genesis 20:11 NIV). Abraham failed, more than once, to stand up boldly for his faith in God, let alone preach a message of faith or salvation.

If you look at Jesus and His disciples, you will note that when He called them, He told them frankly that they were going to be fishers of men (Matthew 4:19). The disciples did, indeed, become preachers of the gospel. What, however, was Abraham's calling? Judging by Genesis 13:2, Abraham's immediate purpose from God was to become "very wealthy."

In part, then, God called Abraham in order for him to follow his dreams and achieve his goals as a businessman. God wanted Abraham to be a role model for future believers to become godly entrepreneurs. Abraham had been waiting seventy-five years for this call, but then God told him that his time had come. At the same time, God was calling Abraham to begin a spiritual journey and a relationship with God even though Abraham, his wife, and his relatives all served other gods at the time.

The call in your life is about the fulfillment of your goals, your dreams, and your salvation.

In life, you simply cannot do anything without a having a vision or giving serious thought to what you want to do. Oftentimes an idea occurs to a person, perhaps through conversation or reflection or even a dream, but pursuing the ideas presents a problem. However, God has called you from the darkness for a purpose, and He wants you to accomplish it. God want you to be succesful physically, materially, spiritually, and in your relationships with other people. In these ways, you will feed your body, soul, and spirit.

The calling stage in a person's life is the starting point of whatever he or she desires to do in life. This calling could be a career, a business, or even starting a family. The calling can come at any time of your life. Some callings come at an early age; others come to people in their old age. Therefore, it is important to be observant and reflective. Many people bury their dreams because of excuses like age or financial circumstances. Allow me to share some prime examples of people who buried their dreams:

SARAH
Sarah did not believe that she would be able to have a baby because of her advanced age. "So Sarah laughed to herself as she thought, 'After I am worn out and my lord [husband] is old, will I now have this pleasure?'" (Genesis 18:12 NIV).

ZECHARIAH
The priest Zechariah, who was John the Baptist's father, likewise had given up on being a parent due to his age. "Zechariah said to the angel, 'How can I be sure of this? My wife and I are very old'" (Luke 1:18 CEB).

KING SAUL
A person's circumstances in life can sometimes make him or her close the book of life prematurely. Some people convince themselves that success for them or their families is impossible because of material poverty or some other disadvantage. This scenario perfectly describes Saul when God appointed him to become the first king of Israel: "Saul replied, 'But I'm only

from the tribe of Benjamin, the smallest tribe in Israel, and my family is the least important of all the families of that tribe! Why are you talking like this to me?'" (1 Samuel 9:21 NLT).

MOSES

When God called Moses to go and lead the Israelites, his first concern was that he was a "nobody" and was therefore unqualified to go to Pharaoh and demand the release of the Lord's people (Exodus 3:11). God told him in verse 12, "I'll be with you" (CEB).

Secondly, after telling God of his inabilities, Moses moves on to talk of his inadequacies. According to Exodus 3:13–22, Moses told the Lord, "I just don't know enough about who you are!" We may feel that we don't know much about where the Lord wants us to lead, or we may think ourselves unprepared for the job. God's response to Moses was to remind him that He is the "I AM"! While Moses might be inadequate, the God who called him and equipped him certainly is not! God was in essence saying to Moses, "Just do as I say, and I will show you who I AM as you need me to."

Thirdly, after the Lord handled all of Moses' other excuses, Moses decided that if he told people he had met personally with God Himself, they would decide that Moses was lying. In other words, no one would believe what he told them (Exodus 4:1–9). Sometimes you will have the same feeling—that the people you are trying to lead are more educated, richer, and more intelligent than you, and this could be a discouragement.

In a last-ditch effort to escape the yoke God intended for him, Moses appealed to some sort of a speech impediment (Exodus 4:10–17). It may be that Moses just thought, and therefore responded, slowly; or it may be that he stuttered.

Whatever the case, Moses tried to use it as an excuse for not doing the will of God. God's response to Moses was that He made man's mouth and He made man's mind, so He was able to give man what he needed when he needed it. Perhaps, like Moses, you are not a good speaker. But God saw what was in Moses, and because of that He didn't listen to Moses' excuses.

God can speak to you about your goals through dreams, visions, friends, or any other means. Your goal might involve a dream job, a successful business, or an artistic creation. Perhaps your goal is to find your partner in life or start a family of your own. Everybody has ideas and goals, but pursuing them is nearly always difficult. However, "with God all things are possible" (Matthew 19:26 ESV); so your choices are often the difference between your dream being an impossibility and becoming a reality.

It has been observed that life is like a dollar bill. The holder of that dollar bill can spend it in any way he or she wants—but only once. When you spend money, you really have only one of two ways to use it: you can waste it, or you can invest it. Some people cannot succeed in life because they choose to waste their lives on the unnecessary. But the person who properly invests his or her life will surely see better results.

There are three categories of people, and only you and God can know to which category you belong:

1. The first category consists of those who receive something and take immediate action.

2. The second category consists of those who hear but choose to discard or hide what they have learned because they don't want to take a risk.

3. The third category, which includes many people, consists of those who hear but procrastinate about what they want to do. Life is full of opportunities; opportunities knock on people's doors every single day. However, because of procrastination, those opportunities are often missed. As the proverb goes, "Opportunity knocks but once."

Abraham's vision and ambition for greater financial success started with his call. Before that, he was likely biding his time, waiting for his father's death to inherit the family wealth. But God told him to leave everything behind and go to a place unknown to him. Your calling, too, might seem far away. Perhaps you can imagine what you want to accomplish and how, but—like Abraham—you cannot yet know where life will lead you or how it will end.

The most serious obstacle that most people today face in reaching their goals is not a matter of money or the economy or the people in their lives; rather, it is procrastination. Procrastination steals your time and your life. Many people always wait until the last minute—a habit that can be dangerous. Do not keep waiting to start your journey toward the goals, ideas, and visions that you want to accomplish in life.

Proverbs 6:4–14 offers an uncompromising indictment of procrastination:

Don't procrastinate
  —there's no time to lose.
5 Run like a deer from the hunter,
  fly like a bird from the trapper!
6 You lazy fool, look at an ant.
  Watch it closely; let it teach you a thing or two.
7 Nobody has to tell it what to do.

8 All summer it stores up food;
   at harvest it stockpiles provisions.
9 So how long are you going to laze around doing nothing?
   How long before you get out of bed?
10 A nap here, a nap there, a day off here, a day off there,
   sit back, take it easy—do you know what comes next?
11 Just this: You can look forward to a dirt-poor life,
   poverty your permanent houseguest!
12 Riffraff and rascals
   talk out of both sides of their mouths.
13 They wink at each other, they shuffle their feet,
   they cross their fingers behind their backs.
14 Their perverse minds are always cooking up something
   nasty, always stirring up trouble. (The Message)
Clearly, procrastination always leads to trouble.

The calling stage in life is similar to the experience of a stranger calling you. As with a stranger's call, you can either heed or reject the call of your goals and dreams. If you respond to the call, you may not know what you are getting into; but you can rest assured that God makes all things possible.

God was a stranger to Abraham because when God called him from his family, he and all his family were idol worshipers. Nonetheless, Abraham took a risk and followed God.

In Matthew 25:14–30, Jesus tells a parable to emphasize the importance of seizing opportunities:

"Again, it will be like a man going on a journey, who called his servants and entrusted his wealth to them. 15 To one he gave five bags of gold, to another two bags, and to another one bag, each according to his ability. Then he went on his journey. 16 The man who had received five bags of gold went at once and put his money to work and gained five bags more. 17 So

THE CALL WITH PROMISE

also, the one with two bags of gold gained two more. 18 But the man who had received one bag went off, dug a hole in the ground and hid his master's money.

19 "After a long time the master of those servants returned and settled accounts with them. 20 The man who had received five bags of gold brought the other five. 'Master,' he said, 'you entrusted me with five bags of gold. See, I have gained five more.'

21 "His master replied, 'Well done, good and faithful servant! You have been faithful with a few things; I will put you in charge of many things. Come and share your master's happiness!'

22 "The man with two bags of gold also came. 'Master,' he said, 'you entrusted me with two bags of gold; see, I have gained two more.'

23 "His master replied, 'Well done, good and faithful servant! You have been faithful with a few things; I will put you in charge of many things. Come and share your master's happiness!'

24 "Then the man who had received one bag of gold came. 'Master,' he said, 'I knew that you are a hard man, harvesting where you have not sown and gathering where you have not scattered seed. 25 So I was afraid and went out and hid your gold in the ground. See, here is what belongs to you!'

26 "His master replied, 'You wicked, lazy servant! So you knew that I harvest where I have not sown and gather where I have not scattered seed? 27 Well then, you should have put my

money on deposit with the bankers, so that when I returned I would have received it back with interest.'

28 "'So take the bag of gold from him and give it to the one who has ten bags. 29 For whoever has will be given more, and they will have abundance. Whoever does not have, even what they have will be taken from them. 30 And throw that worthless servant outside, into the darkness, where there will be weeping and gnashing of teeth.'" (NIV)

Jesus told this story primarily to help us reflect on the ways in which we respond to God's call and to the opportunities that He presents us. Those who are serious will experience life; but if you don't utilize the opportunities in your life, you will find that time passes faster than you think.

According to Genesis 12:1–5, Abraham responded quickly to the call of God:

The LORD had said to Abram, "Go from your country, your people and your father's household to the land I will show you.

2 "I will make you into a great nation,
    and I will bless you;
I will make your name great,
    and you will be a blessing.
3 I will bless those who bless you,
    and whoever curses you I will curse;
and all peoples on earth
    will be blessed through you."
4 So Abram went, as the LORD had told him; and Lot went with him. Abram was seventy-five years old when he set out from Harran. 5 He took his wife Sarai, his nephew Lot, all the possessions they had accumulated and the people

they had acquired in Harran, and they set out for the land of Canaan, and they arrived there. (NIV)

In whatever aspect of life you wish to succeed—business, relationships, or your spiritual life—you need to be serious, responding to your dreams with purpose and conviction.

CHAPTER THREE

THREE REQUIREMENTS OF THE CALLING

God told Abram to leave his country, his people, and his father's family to move to an unknown place; and at the age of seventy-five, Abraham obeyed, leaving his old life behind in company with his own wife and household as well as his nephew Lot (Genesis 12:1, 4).

In His call to Abraham, God mentioned certain specifics: his country, his people, and his father's household. What is their significance? These elements represent the life of unbelief that Abraham was to abandon for the sake of his godly goals. As Deuteronomy 6:5 says, "You shall love the LORD your God with all your heart and with all your soul and with all your might" (ESV). Jesus later reiterated this fundamental principle in Matthew 22:37. This commandment indicates that the calling stage in life requires one's total commitment, dedication, and perseverance. The person who feels God's call must put all of his or her love, soul, and strength into whatever God calls him or her to do in life.

Abraham took action immediately when God called him. He could have told his heavenly Father, "God, I am old, and I don't think I can leave home or my father at this point." However, Abraham exhibited no doubt or procrastination. Like the businessman that he was, he promptly seized the opportunity to which God had called him.

Life Application #1

For you to achieve your goals and dreams in life as Abraham did, it is important for you to see your success in advance rather than focus on the problems involved. You must respond quickly to your vision for what you should, need, or want to do. You must also love God with all of your heart, mind, and soul, and invest that love into your every endeavor. Do not miss any more opportunities in your life because of procrastination, laziness, doubt, or halfheartedness. As Ecclesiastes 9:10 advises, "Whatever your hand finds to do, do it with [all] your might..." (ESV).

Three particular aspects of Abraham's response to God's call helped Abraham to become successful, and these qualities guide us to three principles for success in the calling stage.

1. The calling stage requires complete surrender.

The word surrender is often used by religious leaders and teachers. It is normally interpreted as giving your soul, body, and spirit to God. In other words, to surrender is to let God control your life.

Often the word surrender is used in association with war. If a leader or commanding officer believes that his armies are not strong enough to fight their enemies, he may order the soldiers to surrender. In ancient times, this meant becoming a slave. Nonetheless, in some cases people must fully surrender in order to survive.

For instance, the prophet Jeremiah advised King Zedekiah of Judah, "He who stays in this city shall die by the sword, by famine, and by pestilence, but he who goes out and surrenders to the Chaldeans who are besieging you shall live and shall have his life as a prize of war" (Jeremiah 21:9 ESV). Later Jeremiah informed the king, "Thus says the LORD, the God of hosts, the God of Israel: 'If you will surrender to the officials of the king of Babylon, then your life shall be spared, and this city shall not be burned with fire, and you are your house shall life'" (Jeremiah 38:17 ESV).

When a person surrenders to God but fails to act, money and other wealth will never rain down upon that person. Abraham yielded his personal goals and dreams to God, then demonstrated that surrender through decisive action. Thus, Abraham succeeded in business and in life.

Take a look at your own life. Do you find that you have surrendered to some unprofitable things that are destroying your life? Perhaps you have surrendered to pornography and this has torn your family apart. Maybe you have surrendered to recreational drugs and you are now addicted. If you will surrender to God and your dreams, you will begin to see some positive changes in your life.

What is holding you back? What is keeping you from responding to your visions and goals? Abraham surrendered completely to God's calling. Surrendering yourself to the dreams and plans that God plants in your heart and mind is the beginning of your journey to success. If you find it difficult to surrender, then ask God to help you—because God is your heavenly Father. He assures us in Jeremiah 29:11-14:

"For I know the plans I have for you, declares the LORD, plans for welfare and not for evil, to give you a future and a hope. 12 Then you will call upon me and come and pray to me, and I will hear you. 13 You will seek me and find me, when you seek me with all your heart. 14 I will be found by you, declares the LORD, and I will restore your fortunes...." (ESV)

The book of James also suggests that we are to submit, or surrender, to God. James 4:7 says, "Therefore, submit to God. Resist the devil, and he will run away from you" (CEB). Once again, we see evidence that God desires for us to give our lives and our plans to Him—one hundred percent. James not only touches on the point of surrendering to God, but he also links it with a second command—to resist the Devil. These two commands go hand-in-hand. Surrendering to God is not easy, and the temptation of returning to our own devices will always remain present. However, your goals and dreams are calling you even now; it is never too late to answer.

2. The calling stage requires complete sacrifice.

Before a person is able to surrender completely, there must be a sacrifice. Sacrifice is another vital ingredient for a person to respond successfully to the calling of God and to his or her dreams and goals. What will you sacrifice in order to follow your dreams and passions? You must let something go in order to attain something more valuable.

When God called Abraham, he had to make the sacrifice of leaving his country, his people, and his family. No doubt these things were precious to Abraham, but in order for this seventy-five-year-old man to achieve his goals, he had to make enormous sacrifices. The person who chooses to follow his dreams needs to sacrifice substantial time and resources, certain emotional ties and dependencies, and possibly more, whether materially or spiritually. A person must give up unprofitable ventures in order to accomplish what he or she truly wishes to achieve.

Without sacrifice, there would be little freedom in life. You may have to sacrifice things that are very dear to you in order to attain what might be best for you. According to John 3:16, God even sacrificed His only Son for man: "God so loved the world that he gave his only Son, so that everyone who believes in him won't perish but will have eternal life" (CEB). Jesus sacrificed His life for man so that anyone who believes in Him will have everlasting life. You, too, can make sacrifices—to achieve prosperity and all manner of good things for yourself and your family.

3. The calling stage requires a complete servant's heart.

Possessing a servant's heart plays a vital role in your ability to respond to your dreams and goals in life. Jesus said in Matthew 20:28 that "the Son of Man did not come to be served, but to serve, and to give his life as a ransom for many" (NIV). Many people want to be the boss, but they forget that they must count to one before two. For a person to follow his or her passion and dreams, he or she must first prepare to serve others. As 1 Peter 5:5 says, "Likewise, you who are younger, be subject to the elders. Clothe yourselves, all of you, with humility toward one another, for 'God opposes the proud but gives grace to the humble'" (ESV).

You require training to achieve your goals; and for you to be successful in your training, you will have to humble yourself. Perhaps you feel that you are better than the person for whom you work. If you don't possess a servant's heart, then, you will not complete your training in order to push on successfully toward your dream.

Numerous passages of Scripture teach us that a person must be humble before God and others in order to achieve a higher purpose or standing. Jesus instructed the disciples, according to Matthew 23:10–12:

"Do not be called leaders; for One is your Leader, that is, Christ. 11 But the greatest among you shall be your servant. 12 Whoever exalts himself shall be humbled; and whoever humbles himself shall be exalted." (NASB, emphasis in original)

Similarly, Jesus explained:

"But it is not this way among you, but whoever wishes to become great among you shall be your servant; 44 and whoever wishes to be first among you shall be slave of all. 45 For even the Son of Man did not come to be served, but to serve, and to give His life [as] a ransom for many." (Mark 10:43–45 NASB)

Paul said in Philippians 2:5–8:

Have this mind among yourselves, which is yours in Christ Jesus, 6 who, though he was in the form of God, did not count equality with God a thing to be grasped, 7 but emptied himself, by taking the form of a servant, being born in the likeness of men. 8 And being found in human form, he humbled himself by becoming obedient to the point of death, even death on a cross. (ESV)

James 4:10 teaches simply, "Humble yourselves before the Lord, and he will lift you up" (CEB).

Perhaps you say, "I am not smart enough to accomplish anything great." In the Bible, Moses too expressed insecurity about the Lord's call for him to lead Israel out of bondage in Egypt. God simply asked Moses, "What is that in your hand?" (Exodus 4:2 ESV). The Lord shifted Moses' attention away from his anxiety about the future and suggested that he notice what was right in front of him—a shepherd's rod. God showed Moses that he could use this ordinary staff to perform miracles as a sign for unbelieving people. As Moses' trust in God grew, so did the magnitude of miracles that God worked through His willing servant.

Likewise, you can use your current job and other circumstances to accomplish your goals. Abraham was a shepherd when he was with his family. When he left them, he built his wealth on what little he carried with him. You can either start from the beginning or build on what you have already started. Turn your passion into your profession. Most of us want to work in already-established firms, which can be a good way to start. However, if you feel that you don't enjoy what you are doing, find something about which you are passionate. It might not earn you much—or any—money at the start, but God will provide the right opportunities to allow you to succeed as you utilize your talents and skills properly.

Applying these principles will help you to feed your body, soul, and spirit, which are paramount to your success in life. In particular, if you ignore your spiritual life, you will be find yourself a shell—a dead person walking. From the account of mankind's creation onward, the Bible makes clear that people truly live only because God infuses us with His spirit—the "breath of life" (Genesis 2:7).

Ultimately, you cannot achieve your goal without God any more than you can spell "goal" without the letter G. Always remember this formula for success in the calling stage:

Surrender + Sacrifice + Servant = Perfect Calling

CHAPTER FOUR

THE PROMISE STAGE

When God called Abraham, God made him the following promises (Genesis 12:2–3):

1. "I will make you into a great nation."
2. "I will bless you."
3. "I will make your name great."
4. "You will be a blessing."
5. "I will bless those who bless you."
6. "Whoever curses you I will curse."
7. "All peoples on earth will be blessed through you."
8. "To your offspring I will give this land."

These eight promises represent the sum total of the oath that God made to Abraham.

What is a promise? The dictionary defines "promise" as "an assurance that one will do something or that something will happen" (Concise Oxford English Dictionary, 11th ed.,

Oxford UP, 2008). If you look carefully at God's promises to Abraham, you will note that they are all in the future tense.

"Promise" is a modest, seven-letter word capable of bringing about miraculous results. A promise can be a powerful motivator. For instance, when someone promises you something, you may be encouraged to work harder and do your best because you are pleased to receive whatever that person has promised and wish to show yourself worthy of the promise.

Oftentimes, you probably will not depend heavily on what others have promised you. However, you will more than likely make promises to yourself about things that you want to obtain or accomplish in your life. For your promises to be effective, you need write them down or otherwise record them. Promises are goals that one has to set and then work hard to achieve. Here are some questions to consider when writing down your promises to yourself:

- Why do you have your particular job or participate in the line of work that you do?

- How do you want to see yourself two or five years from now?

- What do you want out of life? What possessions, relationships, and experiences do you want to have?

- What do you want to see happen in your spiritual life?

- How many people are you willing to help in some way?

- Do you want to lead people to Christ? How many? Do you want to learn how to teach or preach?

We cannot know Abraham's exact situation at the time God made the promises to him, but we can see clearly that those promises of God motivated Abraham to leave his old home and to start a new life. No doubt, Abraham left home for these reasons:

- He wanted to be a great nation.

- He wanted to be blessed.

- He wanted his name to be great.

- He wanted to be a blessing to others.

- He wanted all people on earth to be blessed through him.

Your promises or the goals you want to achieve in life should not be focused on you alone. Consider the people you want to support or help when you achieve your goals. God told Abraham that he would be a blessing to others. Write down names of people whom you want to know Christ, and start praying over them. In writing your goals and what you want to accomplish with your life, please don't limit yourself to life's simplicities. Look again at Abraham's promises. God told him that the people of the earth would be blessed through him.

Abraham was seventy-five years old already, yet he did indeed received all of these promises—even those that seemed impossible. Let your goals and what you want to achieve in life motivate you every time you read them. If you show your list to your friends, they may laugh at you because they themselves have failed many times. They might well think that you are out of your mind, but you cannot allow fear of what your peers think to cripple your dreams—and it will, if you permit it to do so.

THE CALL WITH PROMISE

Abraham did not discuss or debate God's promises with his friends, loved ones, and peers. I strongly believe that had he done so, he would have been discouraged by the other people in his life. They would have told him that, at his age, he could not possibly achieve all of those promises. People nearly always see the problems rather than the solution. One defining characteristic of Abraham is that he did not seek to bargain or negotiate with God as far as when he would receive the promised blessings. He simply left: "So Abram went, as the LORD had told him..." (Genesis 12:4 NIV).

Abraham's promises were clearly established by God. Have you clearly written down your goals on paper yet? If not, start doing so now. Recording your goals will motivate you to work harder. Writing down your goals will also help you to know where, when, and how to start accomplishing what you want to do.

Moreover, having clearly defined goals will help you to leave your comfort zone. God's promises to Abraham kept him steady and on course even as they led him away from the familiar surroundings and most of the people he had always known. Writing down your goals and how you want to achieve them can serve as a crucial source of inspiration.

However, in general, avoid overall deadlines and elaborate timetables. Abraham had absolutely no idea when those promises would be fulfilled. Writing down your goals does not mean that they will happen instantly or on your ideal schedule. Abraham did not ask God, "When are You going to give me all that You have promised me?" Rather than question God, Abraham proved willing to work and wait for God's blessings.

These days, people want fast food, fast vehicles, fast answers, and even faster blessings. Rome was not built in a day, however, and a person's goals and dreams will not be realized in a day, either. Hebrews 11:8 says, "By faith Abraham obeyed when he was called to go to a place that he was going to receive as an inheritance. He went out without knowing where he was going" (CEB).

The promise stage is the most difficult stage because you will face many challenges. How long are you willing to wait to see the fruit of your labor? Most people ask themselves, "When and how will these goals turn into money?" This is the stage of life when most people quit. As you are waiting for the promise to become a reality, you must prepare your heart for anything. Other people or your own missteps may frustrate your efforts, and you will almost certainly find yourself disappointed at times because you seem to have spent a lot of time and resources without making any discernible progress. More than likely, you will face many trials; but don't let those problems derail you.

Genesis 12:10–20 details what Abraham went through during this promise stage in his life:

> Now there was a famine in the land, and Abram went down to Egypt to live there for a while because the famine was severe. 11 As he was about to enter Egypt, he said to his wife Sarai, "I know what a beautiful woman you are. 12 When the Egyptians see you, they will say, 'This is his wife.' Then they will kill me but will let you live. 13 Say you are my sister, so that I will be treated well for your sake and my life will be spared because of you."
>
> 14 When Abram came to Egypt, the Egyptians saw that Sarai was a very beautiful woman. 15 And when Pharaoh's officials saw her, they praised her to Pharaoh, and she was taken into his palace. 16 He treated Abram well for her sake,

THE CALL WITH PROMISE

and Abram acquired sheep and cattle, male and female donkeys, male and female servants, and camels.

17 But the LORD inflicted serious diseases on Pharaoh and his household because of Abram's wife Sarai. 18 So Pharaoh summoned Abram. "What have you done to me?" he said. "Why didn't you tell me she was your wife? 19 Why did you say, 'She is my sister,' so that I took her to be my wife? Now then, here is your wife. Take her and go!"

20 Then Pharaoh gave orders about Abram to his men, and they sent him on his way, with his wife and everything he had. (NIV)

Life Application #2

The preceding account describes a serious famine, which must have threatened Abraham's prosperity. Even though, from the beginning, God had offered Abraham many promises, Abraham's success—even his survival—now seemed to be in question. This kind of situation becomes problematic and discouraging for most people. Indeed, sometimes it seems as if life becomes increasingly difficult, the more prepared a person thinks that he or she is for success. Trouble, however, is a part of life, and oftentimes it plays a part in enabling you to receive God's blessings in the proper way and timing.

The famine mentioned in this passage represents anything that brings discouragement about the choices you have made in life. Not only physical hunger but also physical, emotional, and psychological pain may accompany such disappointment.

When Abraham faced this famine, how did he respond to the challenge? He moved to Egypt to search for food. He did not sit about and say, "God, You have promised, so you have to deliver." Instead, Abraham quickly made a decision and tried to find a solution.

If someone makes you a promise, yet things do not work as you expected, that disappointment can lead to discouragement. As a result, you may be tempted to blame the other person. We sometimes blame the people around us to the extent of attacking them verbally or physically. If you have made promises to yourself, then you may blame yourself or accuse yourself of failure. Blaming people will never solve your problem, however; rather, you have to find a way to handle your situation without pointing fingers.

Complaining about circumstances and other people will only make your life worse. Blaming and finding fault with people is part of human nature, but it is not the best way. Do you know how long it took the Israelite nation to travel from Egypt to the Promised Land? It should have taken the children of God only a couple of months, but because of their complaining, the journey took forty years.

Sometimes our friends and loved ones will introduce an idea that we seize and build upon; but then, when things go wrong, we blame others for initiating the idea in the first place. God told Moses and Aaron to rescue the Israelites from slavery. Thereafter, however, when the liberated Israelites were on their way to the Promised Land, life became difficult. The people who were once joyous over being freed from slavery started blaming Moses and Aaron:

And the people complained in the hearing of the LORD about their misfortunes, and when the LORD heard it, his anger was kindled, and the fire of the LORD burned among them and consumed some outlying parts of the camp. 2 Then the people cried out to Moses, and Moses prayed to the LORD, and the fire died down. (Numbers 11:1–2 ESV)

That night all the members of the community raised their voices and wept aloud. 2 All the Israelites grumbled against Moses and Aaron, and the whole assembly said to them, "If only we had died in Egypt! Or in this wilderness! 3 Why is the LORD bringing us to this land only to let us fall by the sword? Our wives and children will be taken as plunder. Wouldn't it be better for us to go back to Egypt?" 4 And they said to each other, "We should choose a leader and go back to Egypt." (Numbers 14:1–4)

Complaining and blaming people will only distract you from moving forward and accomplishing your goals. How did Abraham overcome the trials of the promise stage?

1. Abraham had faith, and you will also need faith.

Hebrew 11:1 says, "Faith is the confidence that what we hope for will actually happen; it gives us assurance about things we cannot see" (NLT). According to Hebrews 11:9, Abraham was accounted as a man of faith: "And even when he reached the land God promised him, he lived there by faith— for he was a foreigner, living in tents. And so did Isaac and Jacob, who inherited the same promise" (NLT). God did not build that mansion for Abraham right away. The patriarch slept in a tent and was willing to wait for God's own timing for that particular promise to arrive. Hebrews 11:10 continues, "Abraham was confidently looking forward to a city with eternal foundations, a city designed and built by God" (NLT). Abraham pictured events in his mind that would one day come to pass.

THE PROMISE STAGE

In other words, you must picture the future success of what you have started and let that faith keep you going every day. During this time, the promise, which is your goal, should be your motivating factor. Picture the promises as if you already possess their blessings—which is exactly what Abraham did. Throughout the promise stage, God is building a foundation for your success in your marriage, your job, your finances, and your business.

It was by faith that the people of Israel went right through the Red Sea as though they were on dry ground. But when the Egyptians tried to follow, they were all drowned.

30 It was by faith that the people of Israel marched around Jericho for seven days, and the walls came crashing down.

31 It was by faith that Rahab the prostitute was not destroyed with the people in her city who refused to obey God. For she had given a friendly welcome to the spies.

32 How much more do I need to say? It would take too long to recount the stories of the faith of Gideon, Barak, Samson, Jephthah, David, Samuel, and all the prophets. 33 By faith these people overthrew kingdoms, ruled with justice, and received what God had promised them. They shut the mouths of lions, 34 quenched the flames of fire, and escaped death by the edge of the sword. Their weakness was turned to strength. They became strong in battle and put whole armies to flight. 35 Women received their loved ones back again from death.

But others were tortured, refusing to turn from God in order to be set free. They placed their hope in a better life after the resurrection. (Hebrews 11:29–35 NLT)

Your faith will carry you through the challenges in life. Jesus said, according to Matthew 17:20, "Truly I tell you, if you have faith as small as a mustard seed, you can say to this mountain, 'Move from here to there,' and it will move. Nothing will be impossible for you" (NIV).

You may ask, "How can I build my faith?" The answer is found in Romans 10:17, which says, "So, faith comes from listening, but it's listening by means of Christ's message" (CEB).

"Faith Knows the Final Score—An Analogy of Faith"

How would you watch a game if you knew beforehand that your team had already won?

A person knew that he was going to miss an important sports event, so he had it recorded to watch at a later time. However, before watching the game, he inadvertently found out that his team had won. How would the news of his team's victory affect his watching of the game?

How would he react if his team played poorly in the first half? Would he get nervous? Not if he was confident about the news he had heard! He would know that a turnaround was on the way. He would have the knowledge and confidence that no matter how bad it may look, something would have to happen to give his team the victory. In fact, instead of becoming nervous, he might well become excited, anticipating that miraculous turnaround moment. He would know that it had to occur because his team had already won!

He has this confidence because he is now watching the game backward—from the perspective of his having already known the outcome. Everything is now being viewed in relation to the knowledge that his team had already won. The only remaining unknown is the manner in which the win will happen. The moment he found out that his team had won, winning stopped being a possibility (a hope), and instead became a known fact, which is the basis of faith. How silly would it be to watch a rerun of a game where you already knew your team had won and still worry about whether or not they will win? (HopeFaithPrayer blog, 5 February 2014 http://hopefaithprayer.com/faith/faith-knows)

The analogy used in the article excerpt above illustrates perfectly how to use faith in your promise stage of life. Likewise, the author of the book of Acts exhorts, "Be encouraged, men! I have faith in God that it will be exactly as he told me" (Acts 27:25 CEB). Faith is the spark that ignites the impossible and causes it to become possible.

In the words of Rick Renner, "When a person's faith is activated, it sets in motion supernatural power that enables that person to do what he normally would never be able to do."

2. Abraham overcame fear, and you must overcome fear.

As you embark on the journey of achieving your dreams and goals, there is a natural fear of failing. The truth is, however, that fear is afraid of faith. If you maintain a strong faith in what you are doing and in what you are going to achieve, fear will run away from your life. Thus, Jesus asked, "'You of little faith, why are you so afraid?' Then he got up and rebuked the winds and the waves, and it was completely calm" (Matthew 8:26 NIV).

There will be a time when you believe that you cannot make it, and you will see much confusion in your life, your family, your workplace, and your business. A time of fear entered the life of Abraham in Genesis 12:1–16. He was afraid that he would be killed because wicked men would covet his wife. Because of that fear, he deceived others into thinking that Sarah was not his wife.

One truth that every Christian should understand, however, is that problems and pains are inevitable in life. Jesus said, according to John 16:33, "I have told you these things, so that in me you may have peace. In this world you will have trouble. But take heart! I have overcome the world" (NIV). God will show up in your struggle—even at the last minute—if you still believe in what you want to do. Fear is an enemy to success, so don't let fear rob you of your joy and your dreams.

Likewise, Deuteronomy 31:6 says, "Be strong and courageous. Do not fear or be in dread of them, for it is the LORD your God who goes with you. He will not leave you or forsake you" (ESV). In a similar vein, God encourages us in Isaiah 41:10 to "fear not, for I am with you; be not dismayed, for I am your God; I will strengthen you, I will help you, I will uphold you with my righteous right hand" (ESV).

When we are facing challenges in life, we tend only to focus on the pain that we are experiencing. Take comfort, though, that God came to Abraham's rescue in Genesis 12:17–19 and restored his faith:

But the LORD inflicted serious diseases on Pharaoh and his household because of Abram's wife Sarai. 18 So Pharaoh summoned Abram. "What have you done to me?" he said. "Why didn't you tell me she was your wife? 19 Why did you say, 'She is my sister,' so that I took her to be my wife? Now then, here is your wife. Take her and go!" (NIV)

The following verses also encourage us to keep our faith in God:

Trust in the LORD with all your heart
and do not lean on your own understanding;
6 In all your ways acknowledge him,
and he will make straight your paths. (Proverbs 3:5–6 ESV)

Those who stand firm during testing are blessed. They are tried and true. They will receive the life God has promised to those who love him as their reward. (James 1:12 CEB)

God is not a man, so he does not lie. He is not human, so he does not change his mind. Has he ever spoken and failed to act? Has he ever promised and not carried it through? (Numbers 23:19 NLT)

The formula for success in the promise stage, then, is this:

Promise = Faith − Fear

CHAPTER FIVE

THE LAW OF BELIEVING

When The law of believing is a powerful rule by which you will maintain the strong beliefs necessary to achieve your goals and dreams. God showed me this law when He told me how Abraham was a success.

The law of believing says, "If you believe, it will work." This general rule leads us to the following set of practical guidelines:

1. Believe in what you think, and think about what you believe.

2. Believe in what you say, and say what you believe.

3. Believe in what you do, and do what you believe.

4. Commit yourself to what you believe, and believe in that to which you have committed yourself.

5. Believe in what you give, and give as you believe. Give your best to those endeavors to which you commit yourself.

6. Surrender to what you believe, and believe in that to which you have surrendered.

7. Sacrifice yourself to what you believe, and believe in that to which you are sacrificing.

8. Serve what you believe, and believe in what you serve.

The word "believes" occurs 244 times across 218 verses in the Greek concordance of the New American Standard Bible. Jesus used the law of believing throughout His ministry on earth. He used this law in both a spiritual and a physical context. The first part of this chapter comprises passages from the Gospel books of the New Testament in which Jesus healed the sick and accomplished other miracles through the law of believing.

Jesus Curses a Fig Tree

> Early in the morning, as Jesus was on his way back to the city, he was hungry. 19 Seeing a fig tree by the road, he went up to it but found nothing on it except leaves. Then he said to it, "May you never bear fruit again!" Immediately the tree withered.
>
> 20 When the disciples saw this, they were amazed. "How did the fig tree wither so quickly?" they asked.
>
> 21 Jesus replied, "Truly I tell you, if you have faith and do not doubt, not only can you do what was done to the fig tree, but also you can say to this mountain, 'Go,

> throw yourself into the sea,' and it will be done. 22 If you believe, you will receive whatever you ask for in prayer." (Matthew 21:18–22 NIV)

The fig tree that Jesus curses in this passage represents the unproductive elements in our lives. Many Christians continue to hold onto a lot of material, emotional, and physical garbage in their lives, and garbage does not produce any fruit. Eliminating this garbage is difficult, but you can release it if you have faith and adopt the stance that certain things to which you cling are not—or are no longer—fruitful in your life. The fig tree could symbolize laziness, gossip, procrastination, addiction, or many other sources of distraction.

Jesus Heals the Blind

> As Jesus went on from there, two blind men followed him, calling out, "Have mercy on us, Son of David!" 28 When He entered the house, the blind men came to Him, and Jesus said to them, "Do you believe that I am able to do this?" They said to Him, "Yes, Lord." 29 Then He touched their eyes, saying, "It shall be done to you according to your faith." 30 And their eyes were opened. (Matthew 9:27–30 NASB)

The two blind men were desperately in need of healing. They cried out to Jesus, and the first question Jesus asked was, "Do you believe that I can help you?" Their response was positive. Even though Jesus could have healed them without asking, Jesus verified verbally that if they believed, He could heal them—because of the law of believing. You have to believe in what you are doing and put all your heart in to it!

Jesus Raises a Dead Girl and Heals a Sick Woman

When Jesus had again crossed over by boat to the other side of the lake, a large crowd gathered around him while he was by the lake. 22 Then one of the synagogue leaders, named Jairus, came, and when he saw Jesus, he fell at his feet. 23 He pleaded earnestly with him, "My little daughter is dying. Please come and put your hands on her so that she will be healed and live." 24 So Jesus went with him.

A large crowd followed and pressed around him. 25 And a woman was there who had been subject to bleeding for twelve years. 26 She had suffered a great deal under the care of many doctors and had spent all she had, yet instead of getting better she grew worse. 27 When she heard about Jesus, she came up behind him in the crowd and touched his cloak, because she thought, "If I just touch his clothes, I will be healed." 29 Immediately her bleeding stopped and she felt in her body that she was freed from her suffering.

30 At once Jesus realized that power had gone out from him. He turned around in the crowd and asked, "Who touched my clothes?"

31 "You see the people crowding against you," his disciples answered, "and yet you can ask, 'Who touched me?'"

32 But Jesus kept looking around to see who had done it. 33 Then the woman, knowing what had happened to her, came and fell at his feet and, trembling with fear, told him the whole truth. 34 He said to her, "Daughter, your faith has healed you. Go in peace and be freed from your suffering."

THE CALL WITH PROMISE

> 35 While Jesus was still speaking, some people came from the house of Jairus, the synagogue leader. "Your daughter is dead," they said. "Why bother the teacher anymore?"
>
> 36 Overhearing what they said, Jesus told him, "Don't be afraid; just believe."
>
> 37 He did not let anyone follow him except Peter, James and John the brother of James. 38 When they came to the home of the synagogue leader, Jesus saw a commotion, with people crying and wailing loudly. 39 He went in and said to them, "Why all this commotion and wailing? The child is not dead but asleep." 40 But they laughed at him.
>
> After he put them all out, he took the child's father and mother and the disciples who were with him, and went in where the child was. 41 He took her by the hand and said to her, "Talitha koum!" (which means "Little girl, I say to you, get up!"). 42 Immediately the girl stood up and began to walk around (she was twelve years old). At this they were completely astonished. (Mark 5:21–42 NIV)

In verse 36, Jesus says not to be afraid, but to believe that their daughter is not dead. Yet in verse 39, the people at the house where the girl is lying down laugh at Jesus. Don't let the negativity of others turn off your belief. They can laugh at you, but if you believe in what you re doing, keep at it and don't give up.

Jesus Heals a Boy Possessed by an Impure Spirit

> When they came to the other disciples, they saw a large crowd around them and the teachers of the law arguing with them. 15 As soon as all the people saw Jesus, they were overwhelmed with wonder and ran to greet him.

16 "What are you arguing with them about?" he asked.

17 A man in the crowd answered, "Teacher, I brought you my son, who is possessed by a spirit that has robbed him of speech. 18 Whenever it seizes him, it throws him to the ground. He foams at the mouth, gnashes his teeth and becomes rigid. I asked your disciples to drive out the spirit, but they could not."

19 "You unbelieving generation," Jesus replied, "how long shall I stay with you? How long shall I put up with you? Bring the boy to me."

20 So they brought him. When the spirit saw Jesus, it immediately threw the boy into a convulsion. He fell to the ground and rolled around, foaming at the mouth.

21 Jesus asked the boy's father, "How long has he been like this?" "From childhood," he answered. 22 "It has often thrown him into fire or water to kill him. But if you can do anything, take pity on us and help us."

23 "'If you can'?" said Jesus. "Everything is possible for one who believes."

24 Immediately the boy's father exclaimed, "I do believe; help me overcome my unbelief!"

25 When Jesus saw that a crowd was running to the scene, he rebuked the impure spirit. "You deaf and mute spirit," he said, "I command you, come out of him and never enter him again."

26 The spirit shrieked, convulsed him violently and came out. The boy looked so much like a corpse that many said,

"He's dead." 27 But Jesus took him by the hand and lifted him to his feet, and he stood up. (Mark 9:14–27 NIV)

In verse 19, Jesus challenges the disciples by calling them an "unbelieving generation" because they tried everything but couldn't drive away the evil spirit. Jesus mentions, in verse 23, that everything is possible to those who believe, but the disciples didn't believe they would be able to solve the problem. As you pursue your goal and dreams, be reminded that Jesus is with you. When the going gets tough, don't believe in your hardship but believe in Jesus—that with Him all things are possible.

Healing the Royal Official's Son

So he came again to Cana in Galilee, where he had made the water wine. And at Capernaum there was an official whose son was ill. 47 When this man heard that Jesus had come [back] from Judea to Galilee, he went to him and asked him to come down and heal his son, for he was at the point of death. 48 So Jesus said to him, "Unless you see signs and wonders you will not believe."49 The official said to him, "Sir, come down before my child dies." 50 Jesus said to him, "Go; your son will live." The man believed the word that Jesus spoke to him and went on his way. 51 As he was going down, his servants met him and told him that his son was recovering. 52 So he asked them the hour when he began to get better, and they said to him, "Yesterday at the seventh hour the fever left him." 53 The father knew that was the hour when Jesus had said to him, "Your son will live." And he himself believed, and all his entire household." (John 4:46–53 ESV)

Oftentimes, people say that seeing is believing. Those around you will not believe your dream. They will discourage you and make you feel you are wasting your time and resources. Jesus says in verse 48 that unless the people see wonders, they will not believe. Some are waiting for you to fail or to prove yourself successful before they will come to you. The man who was in need believed (verse 50), and immediately his son's health began to improve. If God has given you a dream and a vision for your life, then be confident! Believe in your success.

In numerous other verses throughout the Gospels, Jesus speaks of the power and fundamental importance of faith and belief:

"Truly, I say to you, whoever says to this mountain, 'Be taken up and thrown into the sea,' and does not doubt in his heart, but believes that what he says will come to pass, it will be done for him. 24 Therefore I tell you, whatever you ask in prayer, believe that you have received it, and it will be yours." (Mark 11:23–24 ESV)

But when Jesus heard this, He answered him, "Do not be afraid any longer; only believe, and she will be made well." (Luke 8:50 NASB)

And He said to them, "O foolish men and slow of heart to believe in all that the prophets have spoken!" (Luke 24:25 NASB)

Jesus answered and said to him, "Because I said to you that I saw you under the fig tree, do you believe? You will see greater things than these." (John 1:50 NASB)

If you believe in negative thoughts and ideas, negativity will manifest throughout your life; but if you believe in positive outcomes, you will likewise see and receive the positive blessings that God desires for you. If you believe that you cannot succeed in life, then you won't. Therefore, it is of the utmost importance that you monitor your beliefs along the way. The level of your belief, and what you believe, will determine your success or failure.

CHAPTER SIX

THE EXPLAINATION OF THE LAW OF BELIEVING

The story of Joseph in Genesis chapters 37 to 42 is the best example of holding on to what you believe and not letting anyone or any circumstances change you. Joseph saw from the beginning in his dream that he would be more successful than his family. But he encounted a lot of opposition. When he shared his dream with his family, they thought he was joking.

From Scripture we know that there are at least seven different perceptions that various people had of Joseph:

Joesph's father saw him as an adorable son.

Jacob, Joseph's father, loved him dearly but didn't understand when Joseph told him he would be more successful than everybody else.

> "Now Israel loved Joseph more than any of his other sons, because he had been born to him in his old age; and he made an ornate robe for him" ... 10 When he told his father as well as his brothers, his father rebuked him and said, 'What is this dream you had? Will your mother and I and your brothers actually come and bow down to the ground before you?'" (Genesis 37:3, 10 NIV)

His brothers saw him as a useless dreamer.

When Joseph told his brothers about his dream, this is what they told him.

> "Joseph had a dream, and when he told it to his brothers, they hated him all the more. 6 He said to them, 'Listen to this dream I had: 7 We were binding sheaves of grain out in the field when suddenly my sheaf rose and stood upright, while your sheaves gathered around mine and bowed down to it.' 8 His brothers said to him, 'Do you intend to reign over us? Will you actually rule us?' And they hated him all the more because of his dream and what he had said. 9 Then he had another dream, and he told it to his brothers. 'Listen,' he said, 'I had another dream, and this time the sun and moon and eleven stars were bowing down to me.' 11 His brothers were jealous of him, but his father kept the matter in mind." (Genesis 37:5–11 NIV)

The merchant saw him as a slave.

Joseph's brothers sold him to a merchant who was going to Egypt:

> So when the Midianite merchants came by, his brothers pulled Joseph up out of the cistern and sold him for twenty shekels of silver to the Ishmaelites, who took him to Egypt. (Genesis 37:28 NIV)

Potiphar saw him as a useful servant.

> Joseph had been taken down to Egypt. Potiphar, an Egyptian who was one of Pharaoh's officials, the captain of the guard, bought him from the Ishmaelites who had taken him there. (Genesis 39:1 NIV)

Potiphar's wife saw Joseph as a potential boyfriend.

> Now Joseph was well-built and handsome, 7 and after a while his master's wife took notice of Joseph and said, "Come to bed with me!" 8 But he refused. "With me in charge," he told her, "my master does not concern himself with anything in the house; everything he owns he has entrusted to my care. 9 No one is greater in this house than I am. My master has withheld nothing from me except you, because you are his wife. How then could I do such a wicked thing and sin against God?" 10 And though she spoke to Joseph day after day, he refused to go to bed with her or even be with her. (Genesis 39:7–10 NIV)

The prison guard saw him as a prisoner.

> 20 Joseph's master took him and put him in prison, the place where the king's prisoners were confined. But while Joseph was there in the prison, 21 the Lord was with him; he showed him kindness and granted him favor in the eyes of the prison warden. 22 So the warden put Joseph in charge of all those held in the prison, and he was made responsible for all that was done there. 23 The warden paid no attention to anything under Joseph's care, because the Lord was with Joseph and gave him success in whatever he did. (Genesis 39:20–23 NIV)

The cupbearer saw him as a gifted dream interpreter.

> 9 Then the chief cupbearer said to Pharaoh, "Today I am reminded of my shortcomings. 10 Pharaoh was once angry with his servants, and he imprisoned me and the chief baker in the house of the captain of the guard. 11 Each of us had a dream the same night, and each dream had a meaning of its own. 12 Now a young Hebrew was there with us, a servant of the captain of the guard. We told him our dreams, and he interpreted them for us, giving each man the interpretation of his dream. 13 And things turned out exactly as he interpreted them to us: I was restored to my position, and the other man was impaled." (Genesis 41:9–13 NIV)

But God saw him as a prime minister.

> Then Pharaoh said to Joseph, "Since God has made all this known to you, there is no one so discerning and wise as you. 40 You shall be in charge of my palace, and all my people are to submit to your orders. Only with respect to the throne will I be greater than you." 41 So Pharaoh said to Joseph, "I hereby put you in charge of the whole land of Egypt." 42 Then Pharaoh took his signet ring from his finger and put it on Joseph's finger. He dressed him in robes of fine linen and put a gold chain around his neck. 43 He had him ride in a chariot as his second-in-command, and people shouted before him, "Make way!" Thus he put him in charge of the whole land of Egypt. 44 Then Pharaoh said to Joseph, "I am Pharaoh, but without your word no one will lift hand or foot in all Egypt." (Genesis 41:39–44 NIV)

The rest of his family ended up coming before him in search of provision, and later on they also settled in Egypt.

Joseph passed through all of the trials and challenges that came against him, and he surpassed all of the limited perceptions that other people had of him. No one was able to stop him from what God has put in his heart. Joseph saw something bigger waiting for him. He believed in God, and he believed in his dream of being a great leader. For this, God ultimately blessed him:

Joseph named his firstborn Manasseh and said, "It is because God has made me forget all my trouble and all my father's household." 52 The second son he named Ephraim and said, "It is because God has made me fruitful in the land of my suffering." (Genesis 41:51–52 NIV)

Refuse to accept the negative things that people might say about you, and replace those negatives with a positive, winning attitude. If you want to believe in positive things, you have to be vigilant about what you say because even your own words could destroy you. I like the slogan that the football (soccer) team in Accra, Ghana—the Hearts of Oak—adopted for their crest: "Never say die until the bones are rotten." This motto means that no matter how bad things look, anything is possible so long as any vestige of life remains in you.

As Tony Robbins has said, "Identify your problems but give your power and energy to solutions." Therefore, at this juncture, let us review some detailed explanations of each aspect of the law of belief—"If you believe, it shall work":

1. Believe in what you think, and think about what you believe.

What you think every day is important to the course of your life. When you wake in the morning, you should thank God that you have made it to a new day. Many people go to bed with anger or worry because of the situations that they are experiencing. Thinking what is right and positive is the secret of having the best day, every day. The Bible says that the way you think determines how you will act. In the words of Proverbs 23:7, "for as he calculates in his soul, so is he" (ESV, footnote). Consider what you believe to be true and what types of thoughts and behavior would benefit your life.

Most crimes and evil acts result from a failure to think carefully and trust God before acting. As Jesus said:

"Either make the tree good and its fruit good, or make the tree bad and its fruit bad, for the tree is known by its fruit. 34 You brood of vipers! How can you speak good, when you are evil? For out of the abundance of the heart the mouth speaks. 35 The good person out of his good treasure brings forth good, and the evil person out of his evil treasure brings forth evil." (Matthew 12:33–35 ESV)

If somebody says something negative about you but you believe it is not true, you shouldn't worry. If you dwell on it, it will steal your resources, distract you from your goals, and destroy your day.

2. Believe in what you say, and say what you believe.

If you believe in what you think, then talk about it, too. Speak in accordance with your belief. Paul emphasized the importance of this in Romans 10:9–10:

If you confess with your mouth that Jesus is Lord and believe in your heart that God raised him from the dead, you will be saved. 10 For it is by believing in your heart that you are made right with God, and it is by confessing with your mouth that you are saved. (NLT)

Aligning speech and belief is far more difficult for believers than it might sound. James 3:3–8 warns us about the dangers of the tongue:

When we bridle horses and put in their mouths to lead them wherever we want, we can control their whole bodies. 4 Consider ships: They are so large that strong winds are needed to drive them. But pilots direct their ships wherever they want with a little rudder. 5 In the same way, even though the tongue is a small part of the body, it boasts wildly.

Think about this: A small flame can set a whole forest on fire. 6 The tongue is a small flame of fire, a world of evil at work in us. It contaminates our entire lives. Because of it, the circle of life is set on fire. The tongue itself is set on fire by the flames of hell.

7 People can tame and already have tamed every kind of animal, bird, reptile, and fish. 8 No one can tame the tongue, though. It is a restless evil, full of deadly poison. (CEB)

Jesus Himself emphasized the danger that loose and unbelieving speech poses to your soul:

"I tell you, on the day of judgment people will give account for every careless word they speak, 37 for by your words you will be justified, and by your words you will be condemned." (Matthew 12:36–37 ESV)

Don't waste time talking about things you don't believe. Rather, be excited about what you do believe and talk about it. Joseph's family didn't want to hear about his dreams, yet he didn't stop talking about them.

3. Believe in what you do, and do what you believe.

If your beliefs, thoughts, and speech are in sync, then act upon them! As conventional wisdom suggests, "Actions speak louder than words." Ensure that you are translating your beliefs, thoughts, and words into actions because, as the book of James attests, you deceive yourself if you don't walk in accordance with your faith:

> Know this, my dear brothers and sisters: everyone should be quick to listen, slow to speak, and slow to grow angry. 20 This is because an angry person does not produce God's righteousness. 21 Therefore, with humility, set aside all moral filth and the growth of wickedness, and welcome the word planted deep inside you—the very word that is able to save you.
> 22 You must be doers of the word and not only hearers who deceive themselves. 23 Those who hear but don't do the word are like those who look at their faces in a mirror. 24 They look at themselves, walk away, and immediately forget what they were like. 25 But there are those who study the perfect law, the law of freedom, and continue to do it. They don't listen and then forget, but they put it into practice in their lives. They will be blessed in whatever they do. (James 1:19–25 CEB)

Don't keep talking about your dream without doing anything about them. Put your belief into practice! In other words, you have to walk your talk. Whatever, dream you have, you must start and from somewhere. If you have already started, then believe in what you are doing and persevere.

4. Commit yourself to what you believe, and believe in that to which you have committed yourself.

Commitment is important in everything we do. However, most people find it difficult to commit themselves even to endeavors in which they believe. If you think about what you believe, talk about what you believe, and do what you believe, then you must commit yourself to what you are doing. The Bible says in no uncertain terms that we should choose to be cold or hot—not lukewarm:

> "These are the words of the Amen, the faithful and true witness, the ruler of God's creation. 15 I know your works. You are neither cold nor hot. I wish that you were either cold or hot! 16 So because you are lukewarm, and neither hot nor cold, I'm about to spit you out of my mouth. 17 After all, you say, 'I'm rich, and I've grown wealthy, and I don't need a thing.' You don't realize that you are miserable, pathetic, poor, blind, and naked. 18 My advice is that you buy gold from me that has been purified by fire so that you may be rich, and white clothing to wear so that your nakedness won't be shamefully exposed, and ointment to put on your eyes so that you may see." (Revelation 3:14–18 CEB)

Let people see your commitment to what you believe is best. You can't be on again, off again, yet still expect that you will be successful. Put more hours and more of your heart into the endeavors to which God calls you.

5. Believe in what you give, and give as you believe.

If you think, talk, act, and commit yourself in accordance with what you believe, then you must offer your best. Doing your best is always important in life. Don't settle for "good enough"; nor should you compare yourself, favorably or unfavorably, to any other person. Whatever you have committed to, do it to the best of your ability in order to produce the greatest fruits and blessings. As Paul explained in Colossians 3:23–24:

> Whatever you do, do it from the heart for the Lord and not for people. 24 You know that you will receive an inheritance as a reward. You serve the Lord Christ. (CEB)

In 1 Corinthians 9:24–27, Paul drew on the metaphor of athletic competition, to which his primarily Greek audience—whose culture gave birth to the Olympics—could readily relate:

> Don't you know that all the runners in the stadium run, but only one gets the prize? So run to win. 25 Everyone who competes practices self-discipline in everything. The runners do this to get a crown of leaves that shrivel up and die, but we do it to receive a crown that never dies. 26 So now this is how I run—not without a clear goal in sight. I fight like a boxer in the ring, not like someone who is shadowboxing. 27 Rather, I'm landing punches on my own body and subduing it like a slave. I do this to ensure that I myself won't be disqualified after preaching to others. (CEB)

We have already addressed the remaining three aspects of the law of believing—those of surrender, sacrifice, and service—in the context of the calling stage. These last three guiding principles of the law of believing are:

6. Surrender to what you believe, and believe in that to which you have surrendered.

7. Sacrifice yourself to what you believe, and believe in that to which you are sacrificing.

8. Serve what you believe, and believe in what you serve.

The first time I read an article about a sixty-nine-year-old man in India who has thirty-nine wives, ninety-four children, and thirty-three grandchildren—all living under one roof—I thought it was a mind-blowing story. Most born-again believers would condemn that man because the New Testament disapproves of polygamy. At the very least, as a married man, I can testify that it is sometimes difficult to have one wife—so would not life with thirty-nine wives in close quarters be exponentially more trying?

However, according to the article, the members of this household were in fact highly content—one very big, very happy family. No matter your belief or opinion about polygamy, this situation can be explained by the law of believing. This Hindu man believed that he would be able to handle an exceptionally large family; and so he has. He married his first wife at the age of seventeen, and they are still together.

Many famous inventors of technology that we enjoy and take for granted today relied upon the law of believing. Most of them failed many times; but because they believed in what they wanted to achieve, they stayed the course and didn't quit. As Thomas Edison said, "The first requisite for success is to develop the ability to focus and apply your mental and physical energies to the problem at hand without growing weary. Because such thinking is often difficult, there seems to be no limit to which some people will go to avoid the effort and labor that is associated with it."

Pour your belief and focus into what God has called you to do—and then do it!

CHAPTER SEVEN

THE SUCCESS STAGE

The success stage is also called the "celebration stage." Success is not measured by how much money a person has in the bank or how many properties he or she has acquired; rather, success is properly measured according to the magnitude of challenges a person has faced in life and the manner in which he or she has withstood those trials. As God's angel admonishes in Zechariah 4:10, "Do not despise these small beginnings..." (NLT). Once you start celebrating the modest income that you might be earning now and begin to save, you will steadily build your wealth.

The same applies to spiritual wealth. The best way to measure your spiritual growth is to recognize what God is doing or has done for you already. As Jesus explained, greater and lasting prosperity, whether in this life or the next, begins with the way you handle a little wealth now:

> "Whoever can be trusted with very little can also be trusted with much, and whoever is dishonest with very little will

also be dishonest with much. 11 So if you have not been trustworthy in handling worldly wealth, who will trust you with true riches? 12 And if you have not been trustworthy with someone else's property, who will give you property of your own?" (Luke 16:10–12 NIV)

Start speaking positively about what you are accomplishing, even if it is bringing you only a small amount of gain each month. Remember the power and importance of the tongue, according to both the law of believing (part 2) and Scripture:

With the fruit of a man's mouth his stomach will be satisfied;
He will be satisfied with the product of his lips.
21 Death and life are in the power of the tongue,
And those who love it will eat its fruit.
(Proverbs 18:20–21 NASB, emphasis in original)

Speak positive words about your business, your family, and your job, and continue to do so diligently. Recall Ecclesiastes 9:10, as well as part 5 of the law of believing, and devote all of your might and your best efforts to whatever you decide to do. The success stage of life has its own challenges, which can prove deadly. King Solomon, who possessed vast riches yet struggled at times to find spiritual wealth and contentment for his soul, testified to this truth in Proverbs 30:8–9:

Keep deception and lies far from me,
    Give me neither poverty nor riches;
Feed me with the food that is my portion,
9 That I not be full and deny You and say,
    "Who is the LORD?"
Or that I not be in want and steal,
    And profane the name of my God.
    (NASB, emphasis in original)

When you become successful, everything around you will change. This is the beginning of reaping all that you have sown in the promise stage and before. It requires time, effort, commitment, determination, and dedication to reach this point in life. Therefore, it is all too easy to become extravagant and arrogant like the "rich man" from one of Jesus' parables, "who was dressed in purple and fine linen and lived in luxury every day"—but was ultimately condemned to eternal torment (Luke 16:19 NIV).

When Abraham reached the success stage, his life changed completely. Like Abraham, you must be wise in managing both yourself and your newly acquired wealth, or you will soon find yourself returned to material, as well as spiritual, poverty.

Life Application #3

1. Abraham became a public figure.

Struggles are temporary. As Psalm 30:5 reminds us, "For his anger is but for a moment, and his favor is for a lifetime. Weeping may tarry for the night, but joy comes with the morning" (ESV). Abraham had been struggling to find food in Egypt, but now, as Genesis 13:1–2 recounts:

> ...Abram went up from Egypt to the Negev, with his wife and everything he had, and Lot went with him. 2 Abram had become very wealthy in livestock and in silver and gold. (NIV)

At this stage in life, you will likely have more friends as well as more enemies. Most people do not know how to behave toward others during their success stage. Such was the case with Lot, Abraham's nephew, with whom disputes arose as their businesses began to compete. Rather than share in Abraham's newfound prosperity amicably, Lot wanted the best land and resources for himself. Genesis 3–13 continues Abraham's story:

> From the Negev he went from place to place until he came to Bethel, to the place between Bethel and Ai where his tent had been earlier 4 and where he had first built an altar. There Abram called on the name of the LORD.
>
> 5 Now Lot, who was moving about with Abram, also had flocks and herds and tents. 6 But the land could not support them while they stayed together, for their possessions were so great that they were not able to stay together. 7 And quarreling arose between Abram's herders and Lot's. The Canaanites and Perizzites were also living in the land at that time.
>
> 8 So Abram said to Lot, "Let's not have any quarreling between you and me, or between your herders and mine, for we are close relatives. 9 Is not the whole land before you? Let's part company. If you go to the left, I'll go to the right; if you go to the right, I'll go to the left."
>
> 10 Lot looked around and saw that the whole plain of the Jordan toward Zoar was well watered, like the garden of the LORD, like the land of Egypt. (This was before the Lord destroyed Sodom and Gomorrah.) 11 So Lot chose for himself the whole plain of the Jordan and set out toward the east. The two men parted company: 12 Abram lived in the land of Canaan, while Lot lived among the cities of the plain and pitched his tents near Sodom. 13 Now the people of Sodom were wicked and were sinning greatly against the LORD. (NIV)

Jealousy, pride, and other complications can easily get the better of people—even destroy them—during the success stage. Even your friends can place you in peril. Though they may treat you as a god, and you may begin to think that you no longer need God as you did before, you must not be deceived:

"Beware lest you say in your heart, 'My power and the might of my hand have gotten me this wealth.' 18 You shall remember the LORD your God, for it is he who gives you power to get wealth, that he may confirm his covenant that he swore to your fathers, as it is this day. 19 And if you forget the LORD your God and go after other gods and serve them and worship them, I solemnly warn you today that you shall surely perish." (Deuteronomy 8:17–19 ESV)

2. Abraham became a peacemaker.

Abraham could have asserted his claim over the land and fought his nephew; better yet, he should have left him behind from the start. However, Abraham chose to act humbly and maintain a friendly relationship with his nephew. Instead of being proud and acting upon his rights, he chose peace and fellowship over immediate material advantage. In other words, Abraham decided to trust God to protect his success and bring the full blessings of His promises according to His timing.

Many successful people find it easy to forget how and where they started life. They sometimes become proud and turn away from God, whether deliberately or without even realizing it. Remember that not everybody will celebrate with you on your success, either; yet how you treat those people determines whether you will experience the full measure of blessings, material and spiritual, that God desires for you.

If you are kind to others and treat them with respect and love, God will promote you further. On the other hand, James 5:1–6 contains a strong warning for rich oppressors:

> Pay attention, you wealthy people! Weep and moan over the miseries coming upon you. 2 Your riches have rotted. Moths have destroyed your clothes. 3 Your gold and silver have rusted, and their rust will be evidence against you. It will eat your flesh like fire. Consider the treasure you have hoarded in the last days. 4 Listen! Hear the cries of the wages of your field hands. These are the wages you stole from those who harvested your fields. The cries of the harvesters have reached the ears of the Lord of heavenly forces. 5 You have lived a self-satisfying life on this earth, a life of luxury. You have stuffed your hearts in preparation for the day of slaughter. 6 You have condemned and murdered the righteous one, who doesn't oppose you. (CEB)

In an attempt to bring peace to the situation, Abraham told Lot to choose the tract of land where he wanted to settle, and Lot chose the best part of the land. No doubt Abraham had to swallow his pride to make this offer; but, like Abraham, you should always strive to be a peacemaker. It is one of the secrets to growing wealth—including spiritual reward. As Jesus said, "Blessed are the peacemakers, for they will be called children of God" (Matthew 5:9 NIV). Jesus later elaborated on this promise, observing that God Himself treats others with undeserved kindness for the sake of peace: "But love your enemies, do good to them, and lend to them without expecting to get anything back. Then your reward will be great, and you will be children of the Most High, because he is kind to the ungrateful and wicked" (Luke 6:35 NIV).

From Zero to Hero

God wants man to be completely obedient to His command. This fact is quite well illustrated in the story of Abraham. Although Abraham obeyed God's commandment to leave his old life behind, he did not precisely follow God's instructions in Genesis 12:1. Although God had told Abraham to leave his people and his father's household, Genesis 12:4 reveals Abraham's failure: "So Abram went, as the LORD had told him; and Lot went with him" (NIV). Lot wasn't supposed to go with his uncle, but Abraham allowed his nephew to go.

Therefore, only after Lot had parted ways with Abraham did God finally show Abraham everything He had promised him:

> The LORD said to Abram after Lot had parted from him, "Look around from where you are, to the north and south, to the east and west. 15 All the land that you see I will give to you and your offspring forever. 16 I will make your offspring like the dust of the earth, so that if anyone could count the dust, then your offspring could be counted. 17 Go, walk through the length and breadth of the land, for I am giving it to you." (Genesis 13:14–17 NIV)

Lot represents anyone or anything not of God that secretly lingers in our lives and thereby hinders our ability to see and experience the full blessings of God. Like Abraham, you will ultimately have to rid your life completely of such anchors and distractions, for God insists on complete, not partial, obedience.

When you weed out all of those things that are not profitable in your life, you will reap the fruit of your labor. You will witness a significant change in your business, marriage, and life as a whole. As Jesus instructed us, excessive planning and anxiety about the mundane details of life can also be a hidden impediment to God's blessings in your life:

> "Therefore I tell you, do not worry about your life, what you will eat or drink; or about your body, what you will wear. Is not life more than food, and the body more than clothes? 26 Look at the birds of the air; they do not sow or reap or store away in barns, and yet your heavenly Father feeds them. Are you not much more valuable than they? 27 Can any one of you by worrying add a single hour to your life?
>
> 28 "And why do you worry about clothes? See how the flowers of the field grow. They do not labor or spin. 29 Yet I tell you that not even Solomon in all his splendor was dressed like one of these. 30 If that is how God clothes the grass of the field, which is here today and tomorrow is thrown into the fire, will he not much more clothe you—you of little faith? 31 So do not worry, saying, 'What shall we eat?' or 'What shall we drink?' or 'What shall we wear?' 32 For the pagans run after all these things, and your heavenly Father knows that you need them. 33 But seek first his kingdom and his righteousness, and all these things will be given to you as well. 34 Therefore do not worry about tomorrow, for tomorrow will worry about itself. Each day has enough trouble of its own." (Matthew 6:25–34 NIV)

A relationship with God, including regular engagement with His word, makes the crucial difference in your ability to separate worthwhile relationships, activities, and possessions from those that are mere burdens and distractions. Psalm 1 promises that prosperity will follow:

> Blessed is the man
>   who walks not in the counsel of the wicked,

nor stands in the way of sinners,
    nor sits in the seat of scoffers;
2 but his delight is in the law of the LORD,
    and on his law he meditates day and night.
3 He is like a tree
    planted by streams of water
that yields its fruit in its season,
    and its leaf does not wither.
In all that he does, he prospers. (Psalm 1:1–3 ESV)

Psalm 112:1–5 adds:
Blessed is the man who fears the LORD,
    who greatly delights in his commandments!
2 His offspring will be mighty in the land;
    the generation of the upright will be blessed.
3 Wealth and riches are in his house,
    and his righteousness endures forever.
4 Light dawns in the darkness for the upright;
    he is gracious, merciful, and righteous.
5 It is well with the man who deals generously and lends;
    who conducts his affairs with justice. (ESV)

There is no easy stroll to success, and every good thing is difficult to obtain. No one will hand you success. Yet it is never too late to start! Remember, as the proverb goes, a journey of a thousand miles begins with a single step. Don't think too much about that which you have tried and failed; rather, think about what it is still possible for you to do. Don't consult your fears; rather, consult your hopes and your dreams!

Remember this formula:

Calling Stage + Promise Stage = Success Stage

By following this formula, you can make it big in your life on earth. However, you should also consider investing in your eternal spiritual wellbeing—because whatever we acquire here on earth will not last forever. This is precisely why Jesus advised:

"Do not store up for yourselves treasures on earth, where moths and vermin destroy, and where thieves break in and steal. 20 But store up for yourselves treasures in heaven, where moths and vermin do not destroy, and where thieves do not break in and steal. 21 For where your treasure is, there your heart will be also." (Matthew 6:19–21 NIV)

The world perceives success as the attainment of social status, material or financial objectives, or some other useful goal to be achieved within a specified time frame. The way God defines success is far different, however. Success on God's terms does not depend on immediate enjoyment or utility but, rather, on obtaining rewards of infinite, eternal value for both this life and, especially, the life to come.

Regardless of whether the fortune in question is material or spiritual, however, success does not end with simply attaining prosperity. Once wealth has been made, it must yet be maintained. Therefore, the remainder of this book will examine how Abraham grew his wealth while maintaining his relationship with God.

CHAPTER EIGHT

ONE STEP AT A TIME

Material and spiritual wealth do not arrive on a silver platter. The success stage brings its own challenges, which cause most people to stumble because money starts to control them. On the other hand, those who attain new heights in their spiritual lives conform their behavior to God's instruction and example. The Bible tells us that Abraham became very wealthy yet maintained his love for, and relationship with, God. When we achieve success, whether material or spiritual, we need God's help even more than when we first set out on our journey.

Abraham initially left home in response to the call of God; and, as result of that, he ultimately fulfilled that calling. By the time Abraham had reached the success stage, Genesis 24:1 describes him thus: "Abraham was now very old, and the LORD had blessed him in every way" (NIV). Abraham's own servant embellished on this description, saying, "The LORD has blessed my master abundantly, and he has become wealthy. He has given him sheep and cattle, silver and gold, male and female servants, and camels and donkeys" (Genesis 24:25 NIV).

The Bible therefore says that the Lord blessed Abraham in every way, which seems remarkable. Even people who possess enormous wealth in terms of money and property tend to struggle with their health, family, or other aspects of life. Many rich people are not inwardly happy or content in spite of their mansions and their fleets of luxury cars.

Many factors contributed to the immense and continual success that Abraham enjoyed. Before the Lord can bless us as He did Abraham, we must understand certain key aspects of Abraham's life and success.

Life Application #4

1. Think godly.

Abraham did not become wealthy overnight; rather, his path to success took him many years. The experiences and trials that he faced along this journey prepared him well to maintain the prosperity that he finally achieved. He worked hard physically, mentally, emotionally, and spiritually. His success stemmed from his modes of thought. Abraham maintained his positive thinking from the time that God first called him till his final years.

Most people easily lose focus on the goals that are most important to them. Despite a strong start, they finish the race poorly. When people become rich and famous, their thoughts tend to stray from God toward themselves or other people. Even pastors begin to think differently because they see themselves as powerful and invincible. If you forget what God has done for you, you will never remain happy in life.

Living a balanced life, however, will lead to lasting happiness. A balanced life is one in which you tend to the needs of your body, soul, and spirit. If you ignore any of these aspects of your being, you will struggle inwardly even if you convince most of the people around you that you are doing great. Eventually, your imbalance will come to light, as Jesus explained:

> "No good tree bears bad fruit, nor does a bad tree bear good fruit. 44 Each tree is recognized by its own fruit. People do not pick figs from thornbushes, or grapes from briers. 45 A good man brings good things out of the good stored up in his heart, and an evil man brings evil things out of the evil stored up in his heart. For the mouth speaks what the heart is full of." (Luke 6:43–45 NIV)

Abraham's success in life started with his belief in God and His ability to help Abraham achieve his goals. When Abraham was living with his family in Ur, he saw in his mind that God could help him accomplish so much more. He imagined an eternal, godly realm—and then he placed his confidence in that vision (Hebrews 11:10).

Our mind has eyes capable of seeing many things; after all, we often respond to another person's description or explanation of some event or concept with the words "I see." The best part is, those things that we see in our minds can become a reality. Mental images are extremely powerful. Abraham's grandson Jacob would one day create his own successful shepherding business based on a vision that God sent him in a dream, which inspired him to devise a highly effective model for breeding sheep and goats (Genesis 31:10–13).

The question to ask now is: What kinds of images are you painting in your mind every day? Is God part of the picture, or does it only seem to leave room for you and your own fame? Positive thinking includes thinking about what is pure and acceptable to God. The apostle Paul said that before we can see the perfect will of God, we must renew our minds: "Do not be conformed to this world, but be transformed by the renewal of your mind, that by testing you may discern what is the will of God, what is good and acceptable and perfect" (Romans 12:2 ESV).

The human soul connects the body and the spirit. It is home to your mind and emotions, which nourish the soul and flow out to the body and spirit. If your thoughts lead you to grow excited or angry, then your body experiences that emotion; and your body will take one of two types of action, based on what your mind directs it to do: your action will either gratify the body or glorify God. Renewing your mind regularly with the word of God will ensure that you choose the latter and thereby enjoy success in every aspect of life, which is why God told Joshua:

> "This Book of the Law shall not depart from your mouth, but you shall meditate on it day and night, so that you may be careful to do according to all that is written in it. For then you will make your way prosperous, and then you will have good success. 9 Have I not commanded you? Be strong and courageous. Do not be frightened, and do not be dismayed, for the LORD your God is with you wherever you go." (Joshua 1:8–9 ESV)

Spiritual renewal of the mind in God's word is more than a matter of hearing or speaking, however. You must put His truth into practice. Jesus recognized that all too many people talk the talk without walking the walk:

"Why do you call me, 'Lord, Lord,' and do not do what I say? 47 As for everyone who comes to me and hears my words and puts them into practice, I will show you what they are like. 48 They are like a man building a house, who dug down deep and laid the foundation on rock. When a flood came, the torrent struck that house but could not shake it, because it was well built. 49 But the one who hears my words and does not put them into practice is like a man who built a house on the ground without a foundation. The moment the torrent struck that house, it collapsed and its destruction was complete." (Luke 6:46–49 NIV)

Paul, too, exhorted believers to convert right-minded words and thoughts into godly action, saying, "Practice these things: whatever you learned, received, heard, or saw in us. The God of peace will be with you" (Philippians 4:9 CEB).

2. Give thanks to God.

A significant part of our purpose in life is to thank God and show our appreciation to Him for everything that we have and for the trials through which He has carried us. Giving thanks to God ought to be an important part of our daily lives. True, we do have rough days sometimes, but this does not prevent us from thanking God. Do not base your devotion and thankfulness toward God on your immediate circumstances; rather, look to God and thank Him for who He is and what He has done. When you wake up in the morning, the first thing you should do is thank God for the new day. It is the breath of God that keeps us awake. Many people sleep and don't wake up the next day; so if you wake up in the morning, give thanks to the almighty God.

Psalm 118 is one example of a prayer of thanksgiving that you can offer to God:

> Oh give thanks to the LORD, for He is good.
>   for his steadfast love endures forever! …
> 5 Out of my distress I called on the LORD;
>   the LORD answered me and set me free.
> 6 The LORD is on my side; I will not fear.
>   What can man do to me?
> 7 The LORD is on my side as my helper;
>   I shall look in triumph on those who hate me.
> 8 It is better to take refuge in the LORD
>   than to trust in man. …
> 19 Open to me the gates of righteousness,
>   that I may enter through them
>   and give thanks to the LORD.
> 20 This is the gate of the LORD;
>   the righteous shall enter through it.
> 21 I thank you that you have answered me
>   and have become my salvation.
> 22 The stone that the builders rejected
>   has become the cornerstone.
> 23 This is the LORD's doing;
>   it is marvelous in our eyes.
> 24 This is the day that the LORD has made;
>   let us rejoice and be glad in it.
> 25 Save us, we pray, O LORD!
>   O LORD, we pray, give us success!
> 26 Blessed is he who comes in the name of the LORD!
>   We bless you from the house of the LORD.
> 27 The LORD is God,
>   and he has made his light to shine upon us. …
> 29 Oh give thanks to the LORD, for he is good;
>   for his steadfast love endures forever!
>   (Psalm 118:1, 5–8, 19–27, 29 ESV)

In the Old Testament, Hannah was the mother of Samuel, who became a prophet of God. Hannah's prayer of thanksgiving, offered as she dedicated her young son to God's service, included these words of praise:

> "There is none holy like the LORD:
>   for there is none besides you;
> there is no rock like our God.
> 3 Talk no more so very proudly;
>   let not arrogance come from your mouth;
> for the LORD is a God of knowledge,
>   and by him actions are weighed."
> (1 Samuel 2:2–3 ESV)

3. Take care of what you have.

Life is also about taking proper care of whatever comes into your hands. Despite Jesus' admonishment that a little trust must precede great trust (Luke 16:10), we tend to want more—money, possessions, business clients, children, or whatever our hearts desire—before we prove our ability to manage even a small degree of prosperity and success.

We have already discovered how the trajectory of Abraham's life led him from zero—the abandonment of his home and nearly everyone and everything he knew—to all manner of riches. He achieved this through discipline and dedication, including a steadfast relationship with God. Many people, however, climb to some level of success in life; the real difficulty often lies in remaining there. Sometimes we become convinced that greed will help us toward that end, so we resort to dishonesty, ruthlessness, or other dubious means to acquire more wealth. Jesus addressed greed in a story about a rich fool:

Someone in the crowd said to him, "Teacher, tell my brother to divide the inheritance with me."

14 Jesus replied, "Man, who appointed me a judge or an arbiter between you?" 15 Then he said to them "Watch out! Be on your guard against all kinds of greed; life does not consist in an abundance of possessions."

16 And he told them this parable: "The ground of a certain rich man yielded an abundant harvest. 17 He thought to himself, 'What shall I do? I have no place to store my crops.'

18 "Then he said, 'This is what I'll do. I will tear down my barns and build bigger ones, and there I will store my surplus grain. 19 And I'll say to myself, "You have plenty of grain laid up for many years. Take life easy; eat, drink and be merry."'

20 "But God said to him, 'You fool! This very night your life will be demanded from you. Then who will get what you have prepared for yourself?'

21 "This is how it will be with whoever stores up things from themselves but is not rich toward God." (Luke 12:13–21 NIV)

Most people have a similar attitude as this rich man. They strive to achieve material prosperity by any means so that they can simply take life easy; once they attain success, they want to "eat, drink and be merry" because they believe that they finally have enough. It is not bad to enjoy what you have toiled to attain. However, there are three problems if such a mindset controls your entire approach to life:

First, you are selling yourself short if you rest on the laurels of your success. What new goals, great or small, could you still envision and achieve? What further heights of prosperity could you attain, in terms of not only material possessions but also relationships and spiritual blessings, if you do not simply give up? Do not relinquish the mindsets and habits of commitment, surrender, sacrifice, and service that brought you from where you started life to where you now find yourself.

Second, therefore, the attitude of the rich fool is one of self-centeredness—thinking only of yourself instead of what you might offer other people and God. Regardless of whether you have achieved all that you personally want in life, think about how you can share your blessings with others. Let your love for God and others motivate you to maintain and further expand your present wealth in righteous and godly ways—not squabbling over an inheritance as did the man who prompted Jesus to speak the parable. You may die at any time, like the rich fool, and then you will wish you had invested more in your soul and in spiritual wealth.

Third, living an extravagant and careless life can cost you your hard-earned prosperity before you know it. Though at times it may be necessary for a season, you should never be truly content to spend more than what you receive. Don't spend without replacing because if you don't replenish your wealth, it will disappear.

Learning how to manage what you have is therefore vital. From the beginning, God created us to take care of the resources He has entrusted to us, as well as to "be fruitful and multiply" (Genesis 1:28 ESV). God wants us to prosper and multiply in everything we do. He created man to work with Him in the world (Genesis 2:8). God planted a garden and put Adam there to cultivate and maintain it—"to work it and keep it" (Genesis 2:15 ESV). Additionally, Adam and Eve were to "subdue" the earth and "have dominion" over its other creatures (Genesis 1:28 ESV). In other words, God created mankind to manage resources in a position of responsibility that required discipline.

By fulfilling that purpose, we are fruitful and multiply, which allows us to leave an inheritance to our children in accordance with Proverbs 13:22, which says, "A good man leaves an inheritance to his children's children, but the sinner's wealth is laid up for the righteous" (ESV). The wealth of those who ignore other people and God will find its way, sooner or later, into the hands of those who use their blessings wisely.

If you are placed in charge of someone's business—not unlike the way God entrusted Adam and Eve with the garden, and mankind with all the earth—it is important for you to take the best possible care of it. You must manage the business as your own without abusing the workers or wasting the resources. Remember the parable Jesus told about the the servants and bags of gold (Matthew 25:14–30)—God rewards wise investment. The better care you take of what has been entrusted to you, not only preserving but also increasing what you are given, the more God will bless you in turn. If you cannot manage someone else's business wisely, then how will you manage your own when the time comes? Jesus offers so many illustrations about being a good manager because if you administer things well, whether your own or someone else's, you are going to experience more success in life. Here is another parable that Jesus offered about management—specifically, of other people:

> The Lord answered, "Who then is the faithful and wise manager, whom the master puts in charge of his servants to give them their food allowance at the proper time? 43 It

will be good for that servant whom the master finds doing so when he returns. 44 Truly I tell you, he will put him in charge of all his possessions. 45 But suppose the servant says to himself, 'My master is taking a long time in coming,' and he then begins to beat the other servants, both men and women, and to eat and drink and get drunk. 46 The master of that servant will come on a day when he does not expect him and at an hour he is not aware of. He will cut him to pieces and assign him a place with the unbelievers.

47 "The servant who knows the master's will and does not get ready or does not do what the master wants will be beaten with many blows. 48 But the one who does not know and does things deserving punishment will be beaten with few blows. From everyone who has been given much, much will be demanded; and from the one who has been entrusted with much, much more will be asked." (Luke 12:42–48 NIV)

Sometimes we only pretend to do the right thing when people are watching us. Keep in mind, though, that God remains our supervisor at all times: "No creature is hidden from it, but rather everything is naked and exposed to the eyes of the one to whom we have to give an answer" (Hebrews 4:13 CEB).

Abraham's grandson Jacob offers us a perfect example of good stewardship. Before Jacob left his home country to stay with his uncle Laban, his father Isaac blessed him with this prayer:

> "May God Almighty bless you and make you fruitful and increase your numbers until you become a community of peoples. 4 May he give you and your descendants the blessing given to Abraham, so that you may take possession

of the land where you now reside as a foreigner, the land God gave to Abraham." (Genesis 28:3–4 NIV)

God, too, blessed Jacob:

There above it stood the LORD, and he said: "I am the LORD, the God of your father Abraham and the God of Isaac. I will give you and your descendants the land on which you are lying. 14 Your descendants will be like the dust of the earth, and you will spread out to the west and to the east, to the north and to the south. All peoples on earth will be blessed through you and your offspring. 15 I am with you and will watch over you wherever you go, and I will bring you back to this land. I will not leave you until I have done what I have promised you." …

18 Early the next morning Jacob took the stone he had placed under his head and set it up as a pillar and poured oil on top of it. 19 He called that place Bethel, though the city used to be called Luz.

20 Then Jacob made a vow, saying, "If God will be with me and will watch over me on this journey I am taking and will give me food to eat and clothes to wear 21 so that I return safely to my father's household, then the LORD will be my God 22 and this stone that I have set up as a pillar will be God's house, and of all that you give me I will give you a tenth." (Genesis 28:13–15, 18–22 NIV)

Jacob had received blessings from his father and from God; and he had honored God in return, including by dedicating a tenth of all his future income to Him so that he would never forget God's part in his prosperity. Seemingly, Jacob's journey toward success had begun perfectly, and he had taken every measure necessary to start out on the right foot. Then he arrived safely at his uncle's household, and Laban offered him a job. Jacob even fell in love, meeting the woman with whom he wanted to spend the rest of his life!

So Jacob's story should have been smooth sailing from there, right? If he thought so, then he had another thought coming:

> As soon as Laban heard the news about Jacob, his sister's son, he hurried to meet him. He embraced him and kissed him and brought him to his home, and there Jacob told him all these things. 14 Then Laban said to him, "You are my own flesh and blood."
> After Jacob had stayed with him for a whole month, 15 Laban said to him, "Just because you are a relative of mine, should you work for me for nothing? Tell me what your wages should be."
> 16 Now Laban had two daughters; the name of the older was Leah, and the name of the younger was Rachel. 17 Leah had weak eyes, but Rachel had a lovely figure and was beautiful. 18 Jacob was in love with Rachel and said, "I'll work for you seven years in return for your younger daughter Rachel."
> 19 Laban said, "It's better that I give her to you than to some other man. Stay here with me." 20 So Jacob served seven years to get Rachel, but they seemed like only a few days to him because of his love for her.
> 21 Then Jacob said to Laban, "Give me my wife. My time is completed, and I want to make love to her."
> 22 So Laban brought together all the people of the place and gave a feast. 23 But when evening came, he took his daughter Leah and brought her to Jacob, and Jacob made love to her. 24 And Laban gave his servant Zilpah to his daughter as her attendant.

25 When morning came, there was Leah! So Jacob said to Laban, "What is this you have done to me? I served you for Rachel, didn't I? Why have you deceived me?"
26 Laban replied, "It is not our custom here to give the younger daughter in marriage before the older one. 27 Finish this daughter's bridal week; then we will give you the younger one also, in return for another seven years of work."
28 And Jacob did so. He finished the week with Leah, and then Laban gave him his daughter Rachel to be his wife. 29 Laban gave his servant Bilhah to his daughter Rachel as her attendant. 30 Jacob made love to Rachel also, and his love for Rachel was greater than his love for Leah. And he worked for Laban another seven years. (Genesis 29:13–30 NIV)

Laban's treatment of Jacob seems horribly unfair to us today. Indeed, even allowing for the predicament that Jacob had put Laban in by wanting to marry his younger daughter before his elder daughter had a husband, contrary to cultural expectations, the fact remains that Laban deceived Jacob and completely took advantage of him. They had an agreement, and Jacob worked for seven years—seven years!—to marry the woman he loved, only to be given a different woman in disguise.

Most men today, and perhaps even in Jacob's day, would give up at that point. They would likely want to quit their job, abandon the elder sister, and elope with the younger, figuring that it was their right. At the very least, in Jacob's situation, you might have been tempted to complain to God, asking why everything had to be so difficult and insisting upon His promised blessings.

THE CALL WITH PROMISE

However, Jacob did the unthinkable: he was patient enough to see matters through properly and work for another seven years so that no one could claim any wrongdoing on his part. He knew that his boss was dishonest and that he would not remain in that job forever, yet he waited on God's timing.

Therefore, Jacob endured for fourteen years until, one day, he decided that he had sufficient experience to head back to his own country and start his own business. He didn't simply quit and walk away proudly or angrily, however, even though his uncle had cheated him often. Instead, he approached Laban respectfully, held a civil discussion, and kept an open mind instead of insisting on having his way:

> After Rachel gave birth to Joseph, Jacob said to Laban, "Send me on my way so I can go back to my own homeland. 26 Give me my wives and children, for whom I have served you, and I will be on my way. You know how much work I've done for you."
> 27 But Laban said to him, "If I have found favor in your eyes, please stay. I have learned by divination that the LORD has blessed me because of you." 28 He added, "Name your wages, and I will pay them."
> 29 Jacob said to him, "You know how I have worked for you and how your livestock has fared under my care. 30 The little you had before I came has increased greatly, and the LORD has blessed you wherever I have been. But now, when may I do something for my own household?"
> 31 "What shall I give you?" he asked.
> "Don't give me anything," Jacob replied. "But if you will do this one thing for me, I will go on tending your flocks and watching over them: 32 Let me go through all your flocks today and remove from them every speckled or spotted sheep, every dark-colored lamb and every spotted or speckled goat. They will be my wages. 33 And my honesty

will testify for me in the future, whenever you check on the wages you have paid me. Any goat in my possession that is not speckled or spotted, or any lamb that is not dark-colored, will be considered stolen."
34 "Agreed," said Laban. "Let it be as you have said." 35 That same day he removed all the male goats that were streaked or spotted, and all the speckled or spotted female goats (all that had white on them) and all the dark-colored lambs, and he placed them in the care of his sons. 36 Then he put a three-day journey between himself and Jacob, while Jacob continued to tend the rest of Laban's flocks. (Genesis 30:25–36 NIV)

Clearly, even though Laban mistreated Jacob, he realized that his nephew was special—that Jacob was a blessing in his household and business. You, too, can serve as a conduit for God's blessing in your workplace, even if your boss is unpleasant and you would rather be in a different job.

Meanwhile, Jacob continued to learn good management techniques, and he remained open to adjusting his plans and compromising on his immediate desires. Though Jacob wanted to leave and his uncle wanted to pay him to stay, Jacob offered a deal that seemed highly advantageous to Laban. At God's prompting, and without acting unkindly, Jacob saw his uncle's greed as an opportunity After working for his uncle for fourteen years, he had gained much experience, which he could now use to begin his own business without even leaving his current job.

Indirectly and directly, God can inspire our creativity in finding the best path to success. As Jacob later explained to his wives:

THE CALL WITH PROMISE

"In breeding season I once had a dream in which I looked up and saw that the male goats mating with the flock were streaked, speckled or spotted. 11 The angel of God said to me in the dream, 'Jacob.' I answered, 'Here I am.' 12 And he said, 'Look up and see that all the male goats mating with the flock are streaked, speckled or spotted, for I have seen all that Laban has been doing to you. 13 I am the God of Bethel, where you anointed a pillar and where you made a vow to me. Now leave this land at once and go back to your native land.'" (Genesis 31:10–13 NIV)

How, then, did Jacob multiply his flocks? Genesis 30:37–43 explains:

Jacob, however, took fresh-cut branches from poplar, almond and plane trees and made white stripes on them by peeling the bark and exposing the white inner wood of the branches. 38 Then he placed the peeled branches in all the watering troughs, so that they would be directly in front of the flocks when they came to drink. When the flocks were in heat and came to drink, 39 they mated in front of the branches. And they bore young that were streaked or speckled or spotted. 40 Jacob set apart the young of the flock by themselves, but made the rest face the streaked and dark-colored animals that belonged to Laban. Thus he made separate flocks for himself and did not put them with Laban's animals. 41 Whenever the stronger females were in heat, Jacob would place the branches in the troughs in front of the animals so they would mate near the branches, 42 but if the animals were weak, he would not place them there. So the weak animals went to Laban and the strong ones to Jacob. 43 In this way the man grew exceedingly prosperous and came to own large flocks, and female and male servants, and camels and donkeys. (NIV)

Though Jacob had to exercise patience and change his plans many times over many long years, God never neglected Jacob or His promises. God watched all of Jacob's suffering and toil, but He worked it to Jacob's ultimate advantage, bringing him great wealth. God's timing is always best, as He reminds us in Isaiah 55:8–11:

> "For my thoughts are not your thoughts,
> neither are your ways my ways, declares the LORD.
> 9 "For as the rain and the snow come down from heavens
> the heavens are higher than the earth,
> so are my ways higher than your ways
> and my thoughts than your thoughts.
> 10 For as the rain and the snow come down from heaven
> and do not return there but water the earth,
> making it bring forth and sprout,
> giving seed to the sower and bread to the eater,
> 11 so shall my word be that goes out from my mouth;
> it shall not return to me empty,
> but it shall accomplish that which I purpose,
> and shall succeed in the thing for which I sent it." (ESV)

God has a plan for your life if you will trust and depend on Him. The book of Exodus 14:14 promises, "The LORD will fight for you while you keep silent" (NASB). Jacob explained to his wives how God made him rich and successful in spite of his uncle's treatment:

> So Jacob sent word to Rachel and Leah to come out to the fields where his flocks were. 5 He said to them, "I see that your father's attitude toward me is not what it was before, but the God of my father has been with me. 6 You know that I've worked for your father with all my strength, 7 yet your father has cheated me by changing my wages ten

times. However, God has not allowed him to harm me. 8 If he said, 'The speckled ones will be your wages,' then all the flocks gave birth to speckled young; and if he said, 'The streaked ones will be your wages,' then all the flocks bore streaked young. 9 So God has taken away your father's livestock and has given them to me." (Genesis 31:4–9 NIV)

Perhaps you have been working for someone for many years under similar conditions to those in which Jacob labored for his uncle. Working for someone is always a challenge, but remember that your employer offers you the opportunity to build your own knowledge, experience, and wealth if you work from your heart and allow God to fight your battles for you. Jacob adopted a humble and patient attitude, which left him beyond reproach in how he acted toward his uncle. When necessary, he recalled this for his uncle's benefit:

"I have been with you for twenty years now. Your sheep and goats have not miscarried, nor have I eaten rams from your flocks. 39 I did not bring you animals torn by wild beasts; I bore the loss myself. And you demanded payment from me for whatever was stolen by day or night. 40 This was my situation: The heat consumed me in the daytime and the cold at night, and sleep fled from my eyes. 41 It was like this for the twenty years I was in your household. I worked for you fourteen years for your two daughters and six years for your flocks, and you changed my wages ten times. 42 If the God of my father, the God of Abraham and the Fear of Isaac, had not been with me, you would surely have sent me away empty-handed. But God has seen my hardship and the toil of my hands, and last night he rebuked you." (Genesis 31:38–42)

Jacob endured much with his uncle, but he thereby developed his own family, business, and fortune. Instead of running away, lashing out at Laban's servants, or stealing from Laban's flocks, Jacob proved himself a faithful caretaker and shrewd businessman. He remembered that God was watching everything that he did.

Therefore, although Jacob worked hard for the sake of earthly gain and relationships, he did not neglect spiritual wealth. Like Jacob, you must accept the fact that you cannot bring your material possessions or money with you when you die. Even if you live in a ten-bedroom mansion and own a luxury car for every day of the week, you will rest in a six-foot hole when you die. This is why Jesus directed us to store up treasure for ourselves in heaven, not on earth (Matthew 6:19–21).

In order to amass both earthly and heavenly riches, you need not only to invest and spend wisely but also to remember the principles that led Abraham and Jacob to be blessed in every way. If you do not find yourself so blessed, then God is not to blame; rather, you must examine your own thoughts, words, heart, and actions.

Even if you are a believer, perhaps your faith has become too purely intellectual. Maybe you are practicing religion instead of serving the living God. The world holds many things that can grow to be stumbling blocks in our lives and keep us from hearing the voice of the Lord. Abraham and Jacob knew that they needed to keep their hearts and minds inclined toward God; and, as Jacob demonstrated with Laban, they remembered to treat other people with respect and forgiveness.

CHAPTER NINE

ABRAHAM THE FORGIVER

There is an old saying that it is easier to bury a dead body than to bury something in your heart. When a family, a friend, or even a stranger wrongs you, it can be extremely difficult to let go of your hurt feelings and wounded pride. However, forgiveness is crucial to your spiritual walk with God. Unforgiveness can become a fixture or cancer in your soul, holding you back and wreaking enormous destruction in your life. Believers must forgive as God forgives, no matter how difficult that may be.

Abraham loved Lot enough to bring him along on his journey from Ur to a new life, even though God had instructed Abraham to leave his relatives behind. Perhaps Abraham wanted to help Lot start a new life of his own. Maybe he loved Lot too much to leave him in the idol-worshipping land of the Chaldeans.

Unfortunately, once Abraham and Lot began to prosper in their new lives, rivalry and bickering seem to have set in (Genesis 13:7). In your life, you too may find that a family member or friend whom you helped out of love and kindness later turns against you.

Abraham had every reason to cast Lot aside when jealousy and conflict overshadowed their relationship. Instead, however, Abraham forgave Lot, graciously offering Lot his choice of the land to claim as his own. Though Lot less graciously took the best-looking land for himself, still Abraham maintained a heart of forgiveness and kept the peace between them.

Sometimes you will meet people like Lot, who only seem to take advantage of you in return your assistance and kindness. In their selfishness, they quickly forget how you have helped them. Perhaps your spouse, child, parent, cousin, best friend, or coworker is your Lot. His or her lack of gratitude can be painful and offend you, even to the point that you feel betrayed. Such pain is difficult to surrender.

Nonetheless, if you cannot forgive those who wound you severely, your pain and resentment will fester and prove a hindrance to realizing the glory of God fully in your life. This is especially true with regard to close family members who are a part of your household and daily life. Unable to avoid or ignore the person who wronged you, you will find yourself wallowing in your pain, which will eventually tear you apart. According to the first aspect of the law of believing—"Believe in what you think, and think about what you believe"—you can either dwell on your grudge or you can focus on what is profitable and will help you move forward to success.

In order to let your bitterness go so that it no longer distracts and occupies your mind and your heart, you must not only set the injury aside but also forgive the other person. What, though, constitutes forgiveness? Is it enough simply to say, "I forgive you"? Telling the other person that you have forgiven him or her is the beginning of reconciliation, to be sure. However, as we have already discussed, action must follow your words. Abraham enacted his forgiveness of Lot by rescuing Lot when local rulers took his nephew captive:

> The four kings seized all the goods of Sodom and Gomorrah and all their food; then they went away. 12 They also carried off Abram's nephew Lot and his possessions, since he was living in Sodom.
>
> 13 A man who had escaped came and reported this to Abram the Hebrew. Now Abram was living near the great trees of Mamre the Amorite, a brother of Eshkol and Aner, all of whom were allied with Abram. 14 When Abram heard that his relative had been taken captive, he called out the 318 trained men born in his household and went in pursuit as far as Dan. 15 During the night Abram divided his men to attack them and he routed them, pursuing them as far as Hobah, north of Damascus. 16 He recovered all the goods and brought back his relative Lot and his possessions, together with the women and the other people. (Genesis 14:11–16 NIV)

Life Application #5

How can forgiveness help you to build and maintain material and spiritual wealth? Forgiveness is a spiritual offering that opens many doors for you to receive more blessing. By contrast, the Bible says, "the person who hates a brother or sister is in the darkness and lives in the darkness, and doesn't know where to go because the darkness blinds the eye" (1 John 2:11 CEB). Moreover, if you cannot forgive people who have hurt you, it will affect you directly because, as the adage goes, unforgiveness is like drinking poison and expecting your enemy to die.

Forgiveness was thus a central theme of most of Jesus' teachings. He told us, for instance, to love our enemies:

> "You have heard that it was said, 'Love your neighbor and hate your enemy.' 44 But I tell you, love your enemies and pray for those who persecute you, 45 that you may be children of your Father in heaven. He causes his sun to rise on the evil and the good, and sends rain on the righteous and the unrighteous. 46 If you love those who love you, what reward will you get? Are not even the tax collectors doing that? 47 And if you greet only your own people, what are you doing more than others? Do not even pagans do that? 48 Be perfect, therefore, as your heavenly Father is perfect." (Matthew 5:43–48 NIV)

In telling the parable of the unmerciful servant, Jesus observed that God Himself sets the example of unlimited forgiveness toward us and that He expects no less from each of us:

> Then Peter came to Jesus and asked, "Lord, how many times shall I forgive my brother or sister who sins against me? Up to seven times?"
> 22 Jesus answered, "I tell you, not seven times, but seventy-seven times.
> 23 "Therefore, the kingdom of heaven is like a king who wanted to settle accounts with his servants. 24 As he began the settlement, a man who owed him ten thousand bags of gold was brought to him. 25 "Since he was not able to pay,

the master ordered that he and his wife and his children and all that he had be sold to repay the debt.
26 "At this the servant fell on his knees before him. 'Be patient with me,' he begged, 'and I will pay back everything.'
27 The servant's master took pity on him, canceled the debt and let him go.
28 But when that servant went out, he found one of his fellow servants who owed him a hundred silver coins. He grabbed him and began to choke him. 'Pay back what you owe me!' he demanded.
29 "His fellow servant fell to his knees and begged him, 'Be patient with me, and I will pay it back.'
30 "But he refused. Instead, he went off and had the man thrown into prison until he could pay the debt. 31 When the other servants saw what had happened, they were outraged and went and told their master everything that had happened.
32 "Then the master called the servant in. 'You wicked servant,' he said, 'I canceled all that debt of yours because you begged me to. 33 Shouldn't you have had mercy on your fellow servant just as I had on you?' 34 In anger his master handed him over to the jailers to be tortured, until he should pay back all he owed.
35 "This is how my heavenly Father will treat each of you unless you forgive your brother or sister from your heart."
(Matthew 18:21–35 NIV)

Later, in speaking what we now call "the Lord's Prayer," Jesus established the forgiveness of others as one of the most fundamental aspects of a healthy spiritual life and relationship with God:

"This, then, is how you should pray:
'Our Father in heaven,
hallowed be your name,

10 your kingdom come,
your will be done,
on earth as it is in heaven.
11 Give us today our daily bread.
12 And forgive us our debts,
as we also have forgiven our debtors.
13 And lead us not into temptation,
but deliver us from the evil one.'
14 For if you forgive other people when they sin against you, your heavenly Father will also forgive you. 15 But if you do not forgive others their sins, your Father will not forgive your sins." (Matthew 6:9–15 NIV)

Jesus also emphasized that forgiveness is a more important and acceptable sacrifice than any monetary or material offering:

"Therefore, if you are offering your gift at the altar and there remember that your brother or sister has something against you, 24 leave your gift there in front of the altar. First go and be reconciled to them; then come and offer your gift." (Matthew 5:23–24 NIV)

In writing to the church in Corinth, Paul confirmed forgiveness and love as the basic operating principles for believers in responding to wrongdoing. Though an offender faces consequences of some sort, sooner or later, forgiveness must be the order of the day—both to honor God and to prevent evil from gaining any foothold in your life:

But if someone has made anyone sad, that person hasn't hurt me but all of you to some degree (not to exaggerate). 6 The punishment handed out by the majority is enough for this person. 7 This is why you should try your best to forgive and to comfort this person now instead, so that this person isn't overwhelmed by too much sorrow. 8 So I encourage you to show your love for this person. ...

10 If you forgive anyone for anything, I do too. And whatever I've forgiven (if I've forgiven anything [if there was anything to forgive]), I did it for you in the presence of Christ. 11 This is so that we won't be taken advantage of by Satan, because we are well aware of his schemes. (2 Corinthians 2:5–8, 10–11 CEB)

Action speaks louder than words, so forgiving people should occur through words and actions alike. Though Lot had repaid Abraham's good intentions with disagreeableness and greed, Abraham did not give his nephew the silent treatment, nor did he leave Lot to his fate when the four kings took him prisoner. When Abraham heard that Lot was in trouble, he quickly took action because blood is thicker than water and mercy is stronger than hatred.

As the Bible reminds us often, Christ's example is one of love, friendship, and relationship. After all, God sacrificed his own Son to obtain those very things for us:

Dear friends, let's love each other, because love is from God, and everyone who loves is born from God and knows God. 8 The person who doesn't love does not know God, because God is love. 9 This is how the love of God is revealed to us: God has sent his only Son into the world so that we can live through him. 10 This is love: it is not that we loved God but that he loved us and sent his Son as the sacrifice that deals with our sins.
11 Dear friends, if God loved us this way, we also ought to love each other. 12 No one has ever seen God. If we love each other, God remains in us and his love is made perfect in us.13 This is how we know we remain in him and he

remains in us, because he has given us a measure of his Spirit. 14 We have seen and testify that the Father has sent the Son to be the Savior of the world. 15 If any of us confess that Jesus is God's Son, God remains in us and we remain in God. 16 We have known and have believed the love that God has for us.
God is love, and those who remain in love remain in God and God remains in them. 17 This is how love has been perfected in us, so that we can have confidence on the Judgment Day, because we are exactly the same as God is in this world. 18 There is no fear in love, but perfect love drives out fear, because fear expects punishment. The person who is afraid has not made perfect in love. (1 John 4:7–18 CEB)

Abraham demonstrated loving forgiveness in action through his physical intercession on behalf of the captured Lot. When Abraham learned that God was going to destroy Sodom, he interceded with God directly on behalf of his relatives in the city; and because Abraham was a man of faith, God heard his pleas:

> Then the LORD said, "The outcry against Sodom and Gomorrah is so great and their sin so grievous 21 that I will go down and see if what they have done is as bad as the outcry that has reached me. If not, I will know."
> 22 The men turned away and went toward Sodom, but Abraham remained standing before the LORD. 23 Then Abraham approached him and said: "Will you sweep away the righteous with the wicked? 24 What if there are fifty righteous people in the city? Will you really sweep it away and not spare the place for the sake of the fifty righteous people in it? 25 Far be it from you to do such a thing—to kill the righteous with the wicked, treating the righteous

and the wicked alike. Far be it from you! Will not the Judge of all the earth do right?"
26 The LORD said, "If I find fifty righteous people in the city of Sodom, I will spare the whole place for their sake."
27 Then Abraham spoke up again: "Now that I have been so bold as to speak to the LORD, though I am nothing but dust and ashes, 28 what if the number of the righteous is five less than fifty? Will you destroy the whole city for lack of five people?"
"If I find forty-five there," he said, "I will not destroy it." (Genesis 18:20–28 NIV)

Abraham asked three more times, and God agreed that for the sake of only forty-five, thirty, or even twenty righteous people, He would spare Sodom. Then Abraham said, "May the LORD not be angry, but let me speak just once more. What if only ten can be found there?" God replied, "For the sake of ten, I will not destroy it." (Genesis 18:32 NIV)

Abraham cared so much about his nephew that he was willing to bargain with God, albeit in a humble and selfless fashion. People used to talk to God as we now talk to each other. When you adopt a respectfully negotiating stance toward God, as Abraham did on Lot's behalf, you are engaging in what theologians call prayer of intercession.

How often do you intercede for people who have hurt you in the past? The whole city proved not to boast even ten citizens who were holy before the Lord, meaning that ungodliness had overtaken even Lot's own household. Perhaps you have family members who are unbelievers, yet because they have hurt you, you do not trouble yourself to pray for their salvation. We can negotiate and intercede for our loved ones and enemies alike through prayers.

ABRAHAM THE FORGIVER

The role of the prayerful intercessor who mediates between God and other people recurs throughout the Old Testament. Moses offered this prayer on behalf of the Israelites:

> "But I fell on my knees in the LORD's presence forty days and forty nights, lying flat out, because the LORD planned on wiping you out. 26 But I prayed to the LORD! I said: LORD, my Lord! Don't destroy your people, your own possession, whom you saved by your own power, whom you brought out of Egypt with a strong hand! 27 Remember your servants: Abraham, Isaac, and Jacob! Don't focus on this people's stubbornness, wickedness, and sin." (Deuteronomy 9:25–27 CEB)

The prophet Daniel interceded with God on behalf of Israel, including the people of Judah who, like Daniel himself, were captive in Babylon:

> "Then I turned my face to the Lord God, seeking him by prayer and pleas for mercy with fasting and sackcloth and ashes. 4 I prayed to the LORD my God and made confession, saying, 'O Lord, the great and awesome God, who keeps covenant and steadfast love with those who love him and keep his commandments, 5 we have sinned and done wrong and acted wickedly and rebelled, turning aside from your commandments and rules. 6 We have not listened to your servants the prophets, who spoke in your name to our kings, our princes, and our fathers, and to all the people of the land. 7 To you, O Lord, belongs righteousness, but to us open shame, as at this day, to the men of Judah, to the inhabitants of Jerusalem, and to all Israel, those who are near and those who are far away, in all the lands to which you have driven them, because of the treachery that they have committed against you. 8 To us, O LORD, belongs open shame, to our kings, to our princes, and to our fathers,

because we have sinned against you. 9 To the Lord our God belong mercy and forgiveness, for we have rebelled against him 10 and have not obeyed the voice of the LORD our God by walking in his laws, which he set before us by his servants the prophets. 11 All Israel has transgressed your law and turned aside, refusing to obey your voice. And the curse and oath that are written in the Law of Moses the servant of God have been poured out upon us, because we have sinned against him. 12 He has confirmed his words, which he spoke against us and against our rulers who ruled us, by bringing upon us a great calamity. For under the whole heaven there has not been done anything like what has been done against Jerusalem. 13 As it is written in the Law of Moses, all this calamity has come upon us; yet we have not entreated the favor of the LORD our God, turning from our iniquities and gaining insight by your truth. 14 Therefore the LORD has kept ready the calamity and has brought it upon us, for the LORD our God is righteous in all the works that he has done, and we have not obeyed his voice. 15 And now, O Lord our God, who brought your people out of the land of Egypt with a mighty hand, and have made a name for yourself, as at this day, we have sinned, we have done wickedly.

16 "O Lord, according to all your righteous acts, let your anger and your city turn away from your city Jerusalem, your holy hill, because for our sins, and for the iniquities of our fathers, Jerusalem and your people have become a byword [a disgrace] among all who are around us. 17 Now therefore, O our God, listen to the prayer of your servant and to his pleas for mercy, and for your own sake, O Lord, make your face to shine upon your sanctuary, which is desolate. 18 O my God, incline your ear and hear. Open your eyes and see our desolations, and the city that is called by your name. For we do not present our pleas before you because of our righteousness, but because of

your great mercy. 19 O Lord, hear; O Lord, forgive. O Lord, pay attention and act. Delay not, for your own sake, O my God, because your city and your people are called by your name." (Daniel 9:1–19 ESV)

Daniel's prayer is a perfect example of an intercessory prayer, containing all of the important elements. Believers are to approach God on behalf of others in a heartbroken and repentant attitude, recognizing their own unworthiness, and with a sense of self-denial. Daniel understood this well, acknowledging his sinfulness and his unworthiness to demand anything—for we have no rights before God. To this prayer, God responded with mercy through the angel Gabriel (Daniel 9:20–24).

True intercessory prayer seeks not only to know God's will but also to see it fulfilled regardless of whether it costs or benefits us personally. True intercessory prayer seeks God's glory, not our own. God told Abraham from the beginning that he would be a blessing to others; but most people tend to forget about others when times are difficult, as they tend to forget their promises to God once they begin to experience success.

It is time for you to forgive your enemies and receive your blessings from the Lord. Otherwise, you will only stand in the way of God's blessings for you. Abraham's greatest blessings began when he refused to act out of resentment toward Lot and instead demonstrated real love.

To be sure, an unforgiving spirit is a serious sin and should be confessed to God. If you hold resentment or unforgiveness against someone else in your heart, then you are acting in a way that is not pleasing to God, which hinders your prayers and your daily relationship with Him. God will not hear your prayers unless you also show yourself ready to grant forgiveness. As Hebrews 12:14-15 instructs:

Pursue the goal of peace along with everyone—and holiness as well, because no one will see the Lord without it. 15 Make sure that no one misses out on God's grace. Make sure that no root of bitterness grows up that might cause trouble and pollute many people. (CEB)

Now that you know the truth about forgiveness, you must practice it in your life; for Jesus assured us that if you hold others to account in your heart for their wrongdoing, or if you cling to ill will toward others for any reason, you too will be held to account (Luke 12:48). Learn to forgive anyone and everyone. As Paul wrote to the Ephesians, "Be kind, compassionate, and forgiving to each another, in the same way God forgave you in Christ" (Ephesians 4:32 CEB).

Forgiveness is an access code to God. It is the way to develop a deep relationship with God—and the closer you grow to God, the more He will bless you.

CHAPTER TEN

ABRAHAM THE GIVER

*G*iving has become a huge problem for most believers. Many Christians have a lot of questions when it comes to giving an offering or tithes to God. Who should give—the rich, the poor, the healthy, the sick, the employed, the unemployed, the young, the old? How much should they give? When should they give, and how often? Where, and to whom? Above all, why should we give?

Abraham gave a tenth of all his property to the high priest:

Then Melchizedek king of Salem brought out bread and wine. He was priest of God Most High, 19 and he blessed Abram, saying,

"Blessed be Abram by God Most High,
Creator of heaven and earth.
20 And praise be to God Most High,
who delivered your enemies into your hand."

Then Abram gave him a tenth of everything. (Genesis 14:18–20 NIV)

The question is, where did Abraham learn that he ought to do this? Why did he give tithes to the priest? We will address such questions in this chapter.

Life Application #6

Offering sacrifices to God is a practice that started soon after the fall of mankind to sin. Cain and Abel were the first people in the Bible to give offerings to God:

> Now Adam knew Eve his wife, and she conceived and bore Cain, saying, "I have gotten a man with the help of the LORD." 2 And again, she bore his brother Abel. Now Abel was a keeper of sheep, and Cain a worker of the ground. 3 In the course of time Cain brought to the LORD an offering of the fruit of the ground, 4 and Abel also brought of the firstborn of his flock and of their fat portions. And the LORD had regard for [accepted] Abel and his offering, 5 but for Cain and his offering he had no regard. So Cain was very angry, and his face fell. 6 The LORD said to Cain, "Why are you angry, and why has your face fallen? 7 If you do well, will you not be accepted? And if you do not do well, sin is crouching at the door. Its desire is for you, but you must rule over it." (Genesis 4:1–7 ESV)

Nobody handed Cain and Abel a rulebook on giving offerings, yet they offered sacrifices to God according to the kind of work that they did and the kind of wealth that they had. God accepted Abel's offering and rejected Cain's offering because Abel gave God his best.

Likewise, Noah gave acceptable burnt offerings after the flood; and in response, God vowed that He would never again destroy all living creatures:

> Then Noah built an altar to the LORD and took some of every clean animal and some of every clean bird and offered burnt offerings on the altar.. 21 And when the LORD smelled the pleasing aroma, the LORD said in his heart, "I will never again curse the ground because of man, for the intention of man's heart is evil from his youth. Neither will I ever again strike down every living creature as I have done. 22 While the earth remains, seedtime and harvest, cold and heat, summer and winter, day and night, shall not cease. (Genesis 8:20–22 ESV)

Acceptable offerings always touch God's heart and provide openings for God to pour out His blessings. For this reason, God eventually established as a requirement that His children should offer Him the firstfruits of their labor. Even though he lived long before God issued His law to Moses, however, Abraham understood that it was right to give a tenth of everything he had to God's priest.

Jacob continued this practice, promising God a tenth of all the wealth with which God would bless him (Genesis 28:20–22). In exchange for this promise of the tithe and his oath of devotion to God, Jacob expected that God would remain with him and protect him. Sometimes when we are in trouble, we ask God for help, but later, after we have received everything we hoped, we forget to return to God in thanks. Jacob, however,

THE CALL WITH PROMISE

kept his promises to the Lord, and God did not hesitate to remind him of his oath:

> Then God said to Jacob, "Go up to Bethel and settle there, and build an altar there to God, who appeared to you when you were fleeing from your brother Esau."
> 2 So Jacob said to his household and to all who were with him, "Get rid of the foreign gods you have with you, and purify yourselves and change your clothes. 3 Then come, let us go up to Bethel, where I will build an altar to God, who answered me in the day of my distress and who has been with me wherever I have gone." 4 So they gave Jacob all the foreign gods they had and the rings in their ears, and Jacob buried them under the oak at Shechem. 5 Then they set out, and the terror of God fell on the towns all around them so that no one pursued them.
> 6 Jacob and all the people with him came to Luz (that is, Bethel) in the land of Canaan. 7 There he built an altar, and he called the place El Bethel, because it was there that God revealed himself to him when he was fleeing from his brother." (Genesis 37:1–7 NIV)

Later on, when God gave His people a written law in the time of Moses, He specifically addressed tithes and offerings:

> But you shall seek the place that the LORD your God will choose out of all your tribes to put his name and make his habitation there. There you shall go, 6 and there you shall bring your burnt offerings and your sacrifices, your tithes and the contribution that you present, your vow offerings, your freewill offerings, and the firstborn of your herds and flocks. 7 And there you shall eat before the LORD your God, and you shall rejoice, you and your households, in all that

you undertake, in which the LORD your God has blessed you. (Deuteronomy 12:5–7 ESV)

This passage mentions six types of offerings, all to be given with a spirit of rejoicing:

1. Burnt offerings

2. Sacrifices

3. Tithes

4. Special gifts

5. Freewill offerings

6. The firstborn of your herds and flocks

In burnt offerings and sacrifices, the animal served as a substitute; that is, the animal died in place of the sinner. However, the animal was only sufficient as a temporary substitute, which is why sacrifices needed to be offered periodically, on a continual basis. We don't do burnt offerings and sacrifices anymore because Christ served as the ultimate blood sacrifice, once for all of us, when He died on the cross at Calvary. As the book of Hebrews explains, "He doesn't need to offer sacrifices every day like the other high priests, first for their own sins and then for the sins of the people. He did this once for all when he offered himself" (Hebrews 7:27 CEB).

However, tithes, offerings for special occasions, and voluntary ("freewill") offerings remain important today. "The firstborn of your herds and flocks" could be also be classified as a special or freewill offering. You can give the firstborn offering when you reach an important milestone in your

THE CALL WITH PROMISE

---

journey to success—from your first salary or business income, for instance, or upon the birth of a child. In the church, God may also prompt you to give a special offering to support missionaries or to provide for a particular need for certain people in the congregation or wider community. The Bible sets no particular amount for such offerings; you give them of your own free will, as God leads you, and you give what you can. Such offerings are not usually given often, though individuals and churches may vary in this aspect of their giving habits.

In ancient times, much as Cain gave crops and Abel gave livestock, the people paid their tithes and offering in any form available to them. This commonly included sheep, goats, drink, grain, and other plant and animal products of value. The book of 2 Chronicles recounts, "As soon as the command was spread abroad, the people of Israel gave in abundance the firstfruits of grain, wine, oil, honey, and of all the produce of the field. And they brought in abundantly the tithe of everything" (2 Chronicles 31:5 ESV).

Since transportation over long distances was a difficult prospect in those days, the Israelites were permitted to exchange the plant and animal products for currency and offer their tithe in money:

> "And if the way is too long for you, so that you are not able to carry the tithe, when the LORD your God blesses you, because the place is too far from you, which the LORD your God chooses, to set his name there, 25 then you shall turn it into money and bind up the money in your hand and go to the place that the LORD your God chooses." (Deuteronomy 14:24–25 ESV)

Now believers are able to offer their tithes to their local churches, as the physical centers of worship and Christian community life. For the Israelites, however, a central tent or temple served as the center of religious life and tithe collection. The Mosaic law instructed that "then to the place that the LORD your God will choose, to make his name dwell there, there you shall bring all that I command you: your burnt offerings and your sacrifices, your tithes and the contribution that you present, and all your finest vow offerings that you vow to the LORD" (Deuteronomy 12:11 ESV).

The Israelites were instructed to give a portion of their tithes to Aaron, who was the high priest and brother-in-law of Moses (Numbers 18:28). Out of the various tribes of Israel, the Levites were chosen to serve as priests. Therefore, the Levites did not receive the blessing and inheritance of Abraham in the form of land as the other tribes did. Instead God directed, "For the tithe of the people of Israel, which they present as a contribution to the LORD, I have given to the Levites for an inheritance. Therefore I have said of them that they shall have no inheritance among the people of Israel" (Numbers 18:24 ESV).

Such verses, including the following passage in the words of the prophet Nehemiah, clarify that one purpose of tithes and offerings is to ensure sufficient food for the earthly house of God: "[We promise] to bring the first of our dough, and our contributions, the fruit of every tree, the wine and the oil, to the priests, to the chambers of the house of our God; and to bring the Levites the tithes from our ground, for it is the Levites who collect the tithes in all the towns where we labor" (Nehemiah 10:37 ESV).

Thus, the people gave their tithes and offerings so that the priests and their families would have food to eat. In a similar manner, the gifts that believers offer to their churches today are used in part to support the church pastors and staff and their families. This is why Abraham gave a tithe to the priest Melchizedek long before God had established tithing as a firm legal requirement.

Even the Levites, however, were expected to offer tithes. As God directed, according to Numbers 18:26, "Moreover, you shall speak and say to the Levites, 'When you take from the people of Israel the tithe that I have given you from them as your inheritance, then you shall present a contribution from it to the LORD, a tithe of the tithe'" (ESV).

Nonetheless, many Christians today remain uncertain whether they are required to pay ten percent of their income. The Old Testament, as we have seen already, is clear on this point. Deuteronomy 14:22 instructs plainly, "You must reserve a tenth part of whatever your fields produce each year" (CEB). However, some Christians argue that tithes are not mentioned in the New Testament and, therefore, do not apply to followers of Christ.

Such arguments, even when sincere, ultimately prove ill-founded and narrow in their understanding of the Scriptures. Do Christians serve a different God than Abraham did? In his letter to the Galatians—in the New Testament—Paul wrote to the contrary:

Even so Abraham BELIEVED GOD, AND IT WAS RECKONED TO HIM AS RIGHTEOUSNESS. 7 Therefore, be sure that it is those who are of faith who are sons of Abraham. 8 The Scripture, foreseeing that God would justify the Gentiles by faith, preached the gospel beforehand to Abraham, saying [sic], "ALL THE NATIONS WILL BE BLESSED IN YOU." (Galatians 3:6–8 NASB)

ABRAHAM THE GIVER

Later on in the letter, Paul reiterated this point in no uncertain terms:

There is neither Jew nor Greek, there is neither slave nor free man, there is neither male nor female; for you are all one in Christ Jesus 29 And if you belong to Christ, then you are Abraham's descendants, heirs according to promise. (Galatians 3:28–29 NASB)

Does our spiritual relationship to Abraham necessarily translate into an obligation to pay tithes? Jesus' words according to John 8:39 seem to suggest as much: "If you were Abraham's children ... then you would do what Abraham did" (NIV).

Why, then, do we look so hard for excuses to avoid paying the tithe? In this day and age, many people spin, interpret, or debate the Bible in all manner of ways, but ultimately the Bible is clear in its principles and guidance. Moreover, if we don't follow God's instructions and advice, we encounter problems in our spiritual walk with God. As Peter and the other apostles declared in response to interrogation by the high priest, "We must obey God rather than humans!" (Acts 5:29 CEB).

The New Testament is perfectly clear about the importance and benefits of giving. We are to give as we are able. Sometimes that means giving more than ten percent; sometimes that may mean giving less. It all depends on the ability of each believer and the needs of the church. Every Christian should pray diligently and seek God's wisdom in the matter of tithes and offerings.

Tithing is not based on a law limited to one people, time, and place; rather, it's a principle that persists throughout the Bible. Our tithes and offerings represent a way to show our appreciation to God and to honor Him; yet because all wealth and blessings originate with God, we are robbing Him if we neglect our tithes:

> "From the days of your fathers you have turned aside from my statutes and have not kept them. Return to me, and I will return to you, says the LORD of hosts. But you say, 'How shall we return?' 8 Will man rob God? Yet you are robbing me.' But you say, 'How have we robbed you?' In your tithes and contributions.
> 9 You are cursed with a curse, for you are robbing me, the whole nation of you. 10 Bring the full tithe into the storehouse, that there may be food in my house. And thereby put me to the test, says the LORD of hosts, if I will not open the windows of heaven for you and pour down for you a blessing until there is no more need." (Malachi 3:7–10 ESV)

Christianity is not about religion so much as relationship. Because of that, we must always consider the needs of the church and the people around us. Whether the needy are believers or unbelievers, we ought to demonstrate our faith in Christ to them through our loving generosity. Acts 2:45 records that believers "would sell pieces of property and possessions and distribute the proceeds to everyone who needed them" (CEB). Selling your belongings to help someone in need is an even greater sacrifice than paying ten percent of your income.

We can prove our faith in Christ through action in so many different ways. The most common and basic way for us to do so is to show genuine concern over other people's needs. Demonstrating our Christ-like love and compassion for others is not optional, either, for as James declared simply, "faith without works is dead":

> What does it profit, my brethren, if someone says he has faith but he has no works? Can that faith save him? 15 If a brother or sister is without clothing and in need of daily food, 16 and one of you says to them, "Go in peace, be warmed and filled," and yet you do not give them what is necessary for their body, what use is that? 17 Even so faith, if it has no works, is dead, being by itself.
> 18 But someone may well say, "You have faith and I have works; show me your faith without the works, and I will show you my faith by my works." 19 You believe that God is one. You do well; the demons also believe, and shudder. 20 But are you willing to recognize, you foolish fellow, that faith without works is useless? 21 Was not Abraham our father justified by works when he offered up Isaac his son on the altar? 22 You see that faith was working with his works, and as a result of the works, faith was perfected; 23 and the Scripture was fulfilled which says, "AND ABRAHAM BELIEVED GOD, AND IT WAS RECKONED TO HIM AS RIGHTEOUSNESS," and he was called the friend of God. 24 You see that a man is justified by works and not by faith alone. 25 In the same way, was not Rahab the harlot also justified by works when she received the messengers and sent them out by another way? 26 For just as the body without the spirit is dead, so also faith without works is dead. (James 2:14–26 NASB, emphasis in original)

James knew that Abraham experienced an abundance of blessing from God because of his faith expressed through action. In particular, Abraham did not hesitate to obey God and return to Him whatever He asked for—even Abraham's own son! Thankfully, God spared Abraham's son as He spared all of us, Abraham's spiritual descendants, by sacrificing His own Child instead. However, as Jesus made clear in the following parable, God does insist that you provide for those in need:

> "A man was going down from Jerusalem to Jericho, when he was attacked by robbers. They stripped him of his clothes, beat him and went away, leaving him half dead. 31 A priest happened to be going down the same road, and when he saw the man, he passed by on the other side. 32 So too, a Levite, when he came to the place and saw him, passed by on the other side. 33 But a Samaritan, as he traveled, came where the man was; and when he saw him, he took pity on him. 34 He went to him and bandaged his wounds, pouring on oil and wine. Then he put the man on his own donkey, brought him to an inn and took care of him. 35 The next day he took out two denarii and gave them to the innkeeper. 'Look after him,' he said, 'and when I return, I will reimburse you for any extra expense you may have.'
> 36 "Which of these three do you think was a neighbor to the man who fell into the hands of robbers?"
> 37 The expert in the law replied, "The one who had mercy on him." Jesus told him, "Go and do likewise."
> (Luke 10:30–37 NIV)

Churches today invest more in inwardly focused programs and activities than they do in helping the needy. Though such programs might fulfill valid material, social, and spiritual needs, we too often forget those with the most severe needs. People inside as well as outside the church are suffering from physical—and spiritual—pain and hunger. The best way to put your faith into action is to help the needy; then God will richly bless you with eternal rewards. Unfortunately, following the examples of the churches, individual believers also tend to neglect those whom Jesus called "the least of these brothers and sisters of mine":

> "When the Son of Man comes in his glory, and all the angels with him, he will sit on his glorious throne. 32 All the

nations will be gathered before him, and he will separate the people one from another as a shepherd separates the sheep from the goats. 33 He will put the sheep on his right and the goats on his left.
34 "Then the King will say to those on his right, 'Come, you who are blessed by my Father; take your inheritance, the kingdom prepared for you since the creation of the world. 35 'For I was hungry and you gave me something to eat, I was thirsty and you gave me something to drink, I was a stranger and you invited me in, 36 I needed clothes and you clothed me, I was sick and you looked after me, I was in prison and you came to visit me.'
37 "Then the righteous will answer him, 'Lord, when did we see you hungry and feed you, or thirsty and give you something to drink? 38 When did we see you a stranger and invite you in, or needing clothes and clothe you? 39 When did we see you sick or in prison and go to visit you?'
40 "The King will reply, 'Truly I tell you, whatever you did for one of the least of these brothers and sisters of mine, you did for me.'
41 "Then he will say to those on his left, 'Depart from me, you who are cursed, into the eternal fire prepared for the devil and his angels. 42 For I was hungry and you gave me nothing to eat, I was thirsty and you gave me nothing to drink, 43 I was a stranger and you did not invite me in, I needed clothes and you did not clothe me, I was sick and in prison and you did not look after me.'
44 "They also will answer, 'Lord, when did we see you hungry or thirsty or a stranger or needing clothes or sick or in prison, and did not help you?'
45 "He will reply, 'Truly I tell you, whatever you did not do for one of the least of these, you did not do for me.'
46 "Then they will go away to eternal punishment, but the righteous to eternal life." (Matthew 25:31–46 NIV)

CHAPTER ELEVEN

WHY TITHES AND OFFERING

Ultimately, tithing and other forms of giving are not a matter of Old or New Testament teaching but, rather, of the practical application of a basic biblical principle for success. Tithes and offerings are means of investment in God's work—not dissimilar from business investment. Most people resist or avoid giving because they do not see the value of such investment. However, the following verses reveal the magnitude of the returns that you can expect—spiritually as well as, oftentimes, materially and financially—when you apply your resources righteously through faithful giving:

Whoever is generous to the poor lends to the LORD, and he will repay him for his deeds. (Proverbs 19:17 ESV)

Whoever has a bountiful eye will be blessed, for he shares his bread with the poor. (Proverbs 22:9 ESV)

> Cast your bread upon the waters, for you will find it after many days. (Ecclesiastes 11:1 ESV)

> "Give, and it will be given to you. A good measure, pressed down, shaken together and running over, will be poured into your lap. For with the measure you use, it will be measured to you." (Luke 6:38 NIV)

> I'm not hoping for a gift, but I am hoping for a profit that accumulates in your account. (Philippians 4:17 CEB)

> Now this I say, he who sows sparingly will also reap sparingly, and he who sows bountifully will also reap bountifully. (2 Corinthians 9:6 NASB, emphasis in original)

Investment of our resources in the church also serves a practical purpose by supporting church workers. As the Israelites were mindful to support the priests and their families through the ancient tithes, we must not undervalue or overlook the financial needs of those people who devote themselves to the life and mission of the church:

> Elders who lead well should be paid double, especially those who work with public speaking and teaching. 18 The scripture says, Don't put a muzzle on an ox while it treads grain, and Workers deserve their pay.
> (1 Timothy 5:17–18 CEB, emphasis in original)

The apostle Paul, in fact, expresses this theme often, reminding believers that those who receive God's truth should provide for their teachers, sharing all good things with them (Galatians 6:6 NIV). In his first letter to the Corinthians, Paul pointedly reminded believers that God's preachers, teachers, and missionaries ought not to be taken for granted. Though Paul himself opted for a path of self-sufficiency insofar as possible, he asserted that church workers have a practical right to material sustenance from their fellow Christians:

> Don't we have the right to eat and drink? 5 Don't we have the right to travel with a wife who believes like the rest of the apostles, the Lord's brothers, and Cephas [Peter]? 6 Or is it only I and Barnabas who don't have the right to not work for our living? 7 Who joins the army and pays their own way? Who plants a vineyard and doesn't eat its fruit? Who shepherds a flock and doesn't drink its milk? 8 I'm not saying these things just based on common sense, am I? Doesn't the Law itself say these things? 9 In Moses' Law it's written: You will not muzzle the ox when it is threshing. Is God worried about oxen, 10 or did he say this entirely for our sake? It was written for our sake because the one who plows and the one who threshes should each do so with the hope of sharing the produce. 11 If we sowed spiritual things in you, is it too much to ask to harvest some material things from you?
> 12 If others have these rights over you, don't we deserve them all the more? However, we haven't made use of this right, but we put up with everything so we don't put any obstacle in the way of the gospel of Christ. 13 Don't you know that those who serve in the temple get to eat food from the temple, and those who serve at the altar share part of what is sacrificed on the altar? 14 In the same way, the Lord commanded that those who preach the gospel should get their living from the gospel. (1 Corinthians 9:4–14 CEB, emphasis in original)

You are not expected to go and borrow money just for your tithe and offering, however. Everyone is to give according to his or her ability, as the following verses attest:

"Every man shall give as he is able, according to the blessing of the LORD your God that he has given you." (Deuteronomy 16:17 ESV)

The disciples, each according to his ability, determined to send relief to the brethren living in Judea. (Acts 11:29 NKJV)

Furthermore, though you must give out of what God provides you, it should come from your heart. In Paul's words, "A gift is appreciated because of what a person can afford, not because of what that person can't afford, if it's apparent that it's done willingly" (2 Corinthians 8:12 CEB).

For practical purposes, the contributions of wealthy men and women are certainly useful to the church—even from the days of Jesus' ministry, when the wife of King Herod's business manager was among those who supported Christ and His disciples:

Soon afterward Jesus began a tour of the nearby towns and villages, preaching and announcing the Good News about the Kingdom of God. He took his twelve disciples with him, 2 along with some women who had been cured of evil spirits and diseases. Among them were Mary Magdalene, from whom he had cast out seven demons; 3 Joanna, the wife of Chuza, Herod's business manager; Susanna; and many others who were contributing from their own resources to support Jesus and his disciples. (Luke 8:1–3 NLT)

Paul advised the wealthy that generosity was especially imperative for their own spiritual welfare, too, and a wise form of investment in their eternal fortunes:

Tell people who are rich at this time not to be egotistical and not to place their hope on their finances, which are uncertain.

THE CALL WITH PROMISE

Instead, they need to hope in God, who richly provides everything for our enjoyment. 18 Tell them to do good, to be rich in the good things they do, to be generous, and to share with others. 19 When they do these things, they will save a treasure for themselves that is a good foundation for the future. That way they can take hold of what is truly life. (1 Timothy 6:17–19 CEB)

However, the Bible encourages poor believers to give as well, as a thanksgiving for God's blessings, no matter how modest they may seem at the present time. God will provide, as He did for the poor widow who offered hospitality to the prophet Elijah:

So he [Elijah] arose and went to Zarephath. And when he came to the gate of the city, behold, a widow was there gathering sticks. And he called to her and said, "Bring me a little water in a vessel, that I may have drink. 11 And as she was going to bring it, he called to her and said, "Bring me a morsel of bread in your hand." 12 And she said, "As the LORD your God lives, I have nothing baked, only a handful of flour in a jar and a little oil in a jug. And now I am gathering a couple of sticks that I may go in and prepare it for myself and my son, that we may eat it and die."
13 And Elijah said to her, "Do not fear; go and do as you have said. But first make me a little cake of it and bring it to me, and afterward make something for yourself and your son. 14 For thus says the LORD, the God of Israel, 'The jar of flour shall not be spent, and the jug of oil shall not be empty, until the day that the LORD sends rain upon the earth.'" 15 And she went and did as Elijah said. And she and he and her household ate for many days. 16 The jar of flour was not spent, neither did the jug of oil become empty, according to the word of the LORD that he spoke by Elijah. (1 Kings 17:10–16 ESV)

As Mark 12:41–44 recounts, Jesus affirmed that the offerings of the poor represent even greater investments, spiritually speaking, than do the tithes of the rich:

Jesus sat down opposite the place where the offerings were put and watched the crowd putting their money into the temple treasury. Many rich people threw in large amounts. 42 But a poor widow came and put in two very small copper coins, worth only a few cents.
43 Calling his disciples to him, Jesus said, "Truly I tell you, this poor widow has put more into the treasury than all the others. 44 They all gave out of their wealth; but she, out of her poverty, put in everything—all she had to live on." (NIV)

To give cheerfully out of poverty brings the greatest blessings of all. In writing to the wealthy Corinthians, Paul praised the charitable example set by the poorer church communities in northern Greece:

Brothers and sisters, we want to let you know about the grace of God that was given to the churches of Macedonia. 2 While they were being tested by many problems, their extra amount of happiness and their extreme poverty resulted in a surplus of rich generosity. 3 I assure you that they gave what they could afford and even more than they could afford, and they did it voluntarily. 4 They urgently begged us for the privilege of sharing in this service for the saints [believers]. (2 Corinthians 8:1–4 CEB)

As the passage above suggests, attitude is key in giving. The following verses show that this theme is prevalent throughout both the Old and New Testaments:

In Exodus 25:2, God instructs the people to "bring Me an offering. From everyone who gives it willingly with his heart you shall take my offering" (NKJV).

Exodus 35:21 recalls that "they came, everyone whose heart stirred him, and everyone whose spirit moved him, and brought the LORD's contribution to be used for the tent of meeting, and for all its service, and for the holy garments" (ESV).

Deuteronomy 15:10 directly relates cheerful generosity to spiritual blessings and earthly success, exhorting the people, "You shall give to him freely, and your heart shall not be grudging when you give to him, because for this the LORD your God will bless you in all your work and in all that you undertake" (ESV). When the people heeded this command, 1 Chronicles 29:9 says, "[t]hen the people rejoiced because they had given willingly, for with a whole heart they had offered freely to the LORD" (ESV).

In 2 Corinthians 9:7, Paul concisely sums up the principle of giving: "Everyone should give whatever they have decided in their heart. They shouldn't give with hesitation or because of pressure. God loves a cheerful giver" (CEB).

God's love is, after all, the basis of His blessings, including success and wealth of all sorts. Therefore, for their own sakes and others', believers ought to give freely to God and to those in need. Acts 20:35 records Paul's words to the Ephesian church leaders: "In everything I have shown you that, by working hard, we must help the weak. In this way we remember the Lord Jesus' words: 'It is more blessed to give than to receive'" (CEB).

Though the greatest rewards are spiritual, Proverbs 3:9–10 describes in material terms the blessings that follow from faithful giving in tithes and offerings:

Honor the LORD with your wealth
and with the best part of everything you produce.
10 Then he will fill your barns with grain,
and your vats will overflow with good wine. (NLT)

Meanwhile, Proverbs 11:24–25 contrasts the practical benefits of generosity with the poverty that comes from hoarding your wealth:

One person gives freely, yet grows all the richer;
another withholds what he should give,
and only suffers want.
25 Whoever brings blessing will be enriched,
and the one who waters will himself be watered. (ESV)

Not only material riches but also physical health and safety will result from your compassion for the needy, Psalm 41:1–3 tells us:

Blessed is the one who considers the poor!
In the day of trouble the LORD delivers him;
2 the LORD protects him and keeps him alive;
he is called blessed in the land;
you do not give him up to the will of his enemies.
3 The LORD sustains him on his sickbed;
in his illness you restore him to full health. (ESV)

Clearly, the giving of tithes and offerings is not in vain, even from the standpoint of self-interest. As you invest in God's church and His children, remember Jesus' teaching from Luke 6:38—that we will receive in accordance with how we give to others. At first glance, it seems counterintuitive that we would get more in return, the more we give; however, such is the logic of God, and He is trustworthy.

THE CALL WITH PROMISE

Sometimes we may think that pastors and religious leaders, and even the poor, are only abusing the funds that people provide them. While we ought to take an interest in how pastors use church money, it is not our work to cast judgment on where and how our offerings are used. God Himself will deal harshly with any leader who abuses the resources entrusted to them. Ezekiel 34:1–10 offers an ominous warning to those pastors who are irresponsible shepherds for the flocks of believers whom God has placed in their charge:

> The word of the LORD came to me: 2 "Son of man, prophesy against the shepherds of Israel; prophesy, and say to them, even to the shepherds, Thus says the Lord GOD: Ah, shepherds of Israel who have been feeding yourselves! Should not shepherds feed the sheep? 3 You eat the fat, you clothe yourselves with the wool, you slaughter the fat ones, but you do not feed the sheep. 4 The weak you have not strengthened, the sick you have not healed, the injured you have not bound up, they strayed you have not brought back, the lost you have not sought, and with force and harshness you have ruled them. ...
> 10 Thus says the Lord GOD, Behold, I am against the shepherds, and I will require my sheep at their hand [hold them to account for the sheep] and put a stop to their feeding the sheep. No longer shall the shepherds feed themselves. I will rescue my sheep from their mouths, that they may not be food for them." (ESV)

Therefore, stop making excuses not to follow God's commands and Christ's example. Give from your heart in supporting your local church as well as those in your community who are in particular need of your wealth, love, and concern. Not only is reaching out to people in need the the best way to spread Christ's message, but God will also reward you bountifully in every way.

There are so many different ways God can bless you and provide for you that it's impossible to even guess them all. And in my experience, He'll usually do so in a way that surprises you. Increasing your income or bringing you extra money is only one of the ways He can work. He can provide you with a free service that otherwise would have cost you a lot more; He can keep your car from breaking down and costing you a hefty bill; He can keep you from becoming sick or your property from being vandalized.

If you are truly trusting God to provide for you, then you know He can (and will) provide all your needs, even when it seems like you can't afford to tithe. If you stop tithing in order to save money, you immediately stop trusting in God and start trusting in yourself and in the world. Tithing keeps you focused on and trusting in God.

CHAPTER TWELVE

ABRAHAM THE JUST

*T*o be corrupt is to be dishonest, often thoroughly so, "for money or personal gain"—even to the point of being "evil or morally depraved" (Concise Oxford English Dictionary, 11th ed., Oxford UP, 2008). In other words, it is money or a favor given or promised in order to influence the judgment or conduct of a person in a trusted position.

We live in a society in which various forms of bribery and embezzlement run rampant. Although corruption has become integrated into business culture, especially, it is important for believers to know that engaging in bribes will lead to serious material and spiritual damage. Those who receive bribes face the same consequences as those who offer them. Unfortunately, most people would accept a bribe because it seems like easy money; and those who pay bribes tell themselves that it's simply a means to get things done quickly.

Abraham, however, refused to accept a bribe from the king of Sodom. He upheld justice, which means that everyone should receive what he or she is due—no more, no less. Here is how Abraham handled things justly when the king offered him a bribe:

> The king of Sodom said to Abram, "Give me the people and keep the goods for yourself."
>
> 22 But Abram said to the king of Sodom, "With raised hand I have sworn an oath to the LORD, God Most High, Creator of heaven and earth, 23 that I will accept nothing belonging to you, not even a thread or the strap of a sandal, so that you will never be able to say, 'I made Abram rich.' 24 I will accept nothing but what my men have eaten and the share that belongs to the men who went with me—to Aner, Eshkol and Mamre. Let them have their share." (Genesis 14:21–24 NIV)

Contrast Abraham's commitment to justice with the corruption that the prophet Samuel's sons practiced as judges, or rulers, of God's people:

> When Samuel became old, he made his sons judges over Israel. 2 The name of his firstborn son was Joel, and the name of his second, Abijah; they were judges in Beersheba. 3 Yet his sons did not walk in his ways but turned aside after gain. They took bribes and perverted justice. (1 Samuel 8:1–3 ESV)

Life Application #7

Perhaps you are saying to yourself even now that you would never accept or offer a bribe; but anyone who doesn't depend on God for strength can fall into the trap of corruption. Abraham refused the bribe from the king because he remembered that God was his provider.

Sooner or later, participation in bribery or other forms of corruption and sin will catch up with you. The book of Acts records the story of Ananias and his wife Sapphira, believers who decided to sell some of their land for the church but then, out of greed, secretly chose to keep some of the money for themselves:

> However, a man named Ananias, along with his wife Sapphira, sold a piece of property. 2 With his wife's knowledge, he withheld some of the proceeds from the sale. He brought the rest and placed it in the care and under the authority of the apostles. 3 Peter asked, "Ananias, how is it that Satan has influenced you to lie to the Holy Spirit by withholding some of the proceeds from the sale of your land? 4 Wasn't that property yours to keep? After you sold it, wasn't the money yours to do with whatever you wanted? What made you think of such a thing? You haven't lied to other people but to God." 5 When Ananias heard these words, he dropped dead. Everyone who heard this conversation was terrified. 6 Some young men stood up, wrapped up his body, carried him out, and buried him. 7 About three hours later, his wife entered, but she didn't know what had happened to her husband. 8 Peter asked her, "Tell me, did you and your husband receive this price for the field?"
> She responded, "Yes, that's the amount."
> 9 He replied, "How could you scheme with each other to challenge the Lord's Spirit? Look! The feet of those who buried your husband are at the door. They will carry you out too." 10 At that very moment, she dropped dead at his feet. When they young men entered and found her dead, they carried her out and buried her with her husband. 11

Trepidation and dread seized the whole church and all who had heard what had happened. (Acts 5:1–11 CEB)

What happened to Ananias and his wife Sapphira could happen to anyone who is likewise greedy and selfish—perhaps not so immediately, yet often as abruptly. Lying and taking advantage of others for the sake of material gain ultimately undermines whatever you hope to accomplish. Since Abraham valued what God had given him, he refused to accept a bribe. To maintain your wealth, you too must know how to distinguish good money from bad.

Each step you take down the path of corruption could be the one that sends you to jail or otherwise destroys your life, costing you even your honestly earned success. You will not find lasting blessings, whether material or spiritual, lying along a quick and easy road. Therefore, avoid shortcuts to the accumulation of wealth. By contrast, justice and integrity—the wholeness and purity of your character and your soul—protect and enhance your good name in the sight of God, which is the best way to safeguard your wealth.

The Roman soldiers who guarded Jesus' tomb were bribed to lie about what had happened to Jesus' body after He rose from the dead. For quick money and to avoid trouble, these soldiers tried to hide the truth about the most important event in all human history; and their corruption is now recorded for all time:

When the chief priests had met with the elders and devised a plan, they gave the soldiers a large sum of money, 13 telling them, "You are to say, 'His disciples came during the night and stole him away while we were asleep.' 14 If this report gets to the governor, we will satisfy him and keep you out of trouble." 15 So the soldiers took the money and did as they were instructed. And this story has been widely circulated among the Jews to this very day. (Matthew 28:12–15 NIV)

Bribery and corruption could also take the form of illicit favors, sometimes including sexual relations, in exchange for information or for career advancement. We see the danger of such corruption in the story of Samson, who was one of the most famous military leaders of Israel prior to God appointing Saul as the first king. Though Samson was a mighty warrior of incredible strength, he sacrificed the purity of his body and soul to a woman and was thereby destroyed:

> After this he loved a woman in the Valley of Sorek, whose name was Delilah. 5 And the lords of the Philistines came up to her and said to her, "Seduce him, and see where his great strength lies, and by what means we may overpower him, that we may bind him to humble him. And we will each give you 1,100 pieces of silver." 6 So Delilah said to Samson, "Please tell me where your great strength lies, and how you might be bound, that one could subdue you."
> 7 Samson said to her, "If they bind me with seven fresh bowstrings that have not been dried, then I shall become weak and be like any other man." 8 Then the lords of the Philistines brought up to her seven fresh bowstrings that had not been dried, and she bound him with them. 9 Now she had men lying in ambush in an inner chamber. And she said to him, "The Philistines are upon you, Samson!" But he snapped the bowstrings, as a thread of flax snaps when it touches the fire. So the secret of his strength was not known.
> 10 Then Delilah said to Samson, "Behold, you have mocked me and told me lies. Please tell me how you might be bound." 11 And he said to her, "If they bind me with new ropes that have not been used, then I shall become weak

and be like any other man." 12 So Delilah took new ropes and bound him with them and said to him, "The Philistines are upon you, Samson!" And the men lying in ambush were in an inner chamber. But he snapped the ropes off his arms like a thread.

13 Then Delilah said to Samson, "Until now you have mocked me and told me lies. Tell me how you might be bound." And he said to her, "If you weave the seven locks of my head with the web and fasten it tight with the pin, then I shall become weak and be like any other man." 14 So while he slept, Delilah took the seven locks of his head and wove them into the web. And she made them tight with the pin and said to him, "The Philistines are upon you, Samson!" But he awoke from his sleep and pulled away the pin, the loom, and the web.

15 And she said to him, "How can you say, 'I love you,' when your heart is not with me? You have mocked me these three times, and you have not told me where your great strength lies." 16 And when she pressed him hard with her words day after day, and urged him, his soul was vexed to death. 17 And he told her all his heart, and said to her, "A razor has never come upon my head, for I have been a Nazirite to God from my mother's womb. If my head is shaved, then my strength will leave me, and I shall become weak and be like any other man."

18 When Delilah saw that he had told her all his heart, she sent and called the lords of the Philistines, saying, "Come up again, for he has told me all his heart." Then the lords of the Philistines came up to her and brought the money in their hands. 19 She made him sleep on her knees. And she called a man and had him shave off the seven locks of his head. Then she began to torment him, and his strength left him. 20 And she said, "The Philistines are upon you, Samson!" And he awoke from his sleep and said, "I will go out as at other times and shake myself free." But he did not

know that the LORD had left him. 21 And the Philistines seized him and gouged out his eyes and brought him down to Gaza and bound him with bronze shackles. And he ground at the mill in the prison. (Judges 16:4–21 ESV)

Another New Testament example of bribery is found in Acts. Simon the sorcerer saw the apostles Peter and John lay their hands on some Samaritan believers, and the Samaritans received the Holy Spirit. Simon was so desirous of the apostles' power that he tried to bribe them into giving it to him:

"But Peter said to him, 'May your silver perish with you, because you thought you could obtain the gift of God with money! 21 You have no part or portion in this matter, for your heart is not right before God. 22 Therefore repent of this wickedness of yours, and pray to the Lord that, if possible, the intent of your heart may be forgiven you. 23 For I see that you are in the gall of bitterness and in the bondage of iniquity.'" (Acts 8:20–23 NASB)

Those who would offer or receive bribes are involved in wickedness. Though specifics may change across time and place, the problems that beset people in the Bible still afflict our society today. Don't look for shortcuts to prosperity; doing so leads to death—whether yours or someone else's, either in this life or the next, if not all of these. According to the words of Jesus in Matthew 7:13–14:

"Enter through the narrow gate. For wide is the gate and broad is the road that leads to destruction, and many enter through it. 14 But small is the gate and narrow the road that leads to life, and only a few find it." (NIV)

The book of Proverbs assures us, "There is a way that seems right to a man, but its end is the way to death" (Proverbs

14:12 ESV). Rather, we are to act honestly and justly: "Whoever walks in uprightness fears the LORD, but he who is devious in his ways despises him" (Proverbs 14:2 ESV). For our own sakes, then, the following scriptures steer us firmly away from the unjust practice of bribery:

"For the LORD your God is God of gods and Lord of lords, the great, the mighty, and the awesome God, who is not partial and takes no bribe." (Deuteronomy 10:17 ESV)

"And you shall take no bribe, for a bribe blinds the clear-sighted and subverts the cause of those who are in the right." (Exodus 23:8 ESV)

"You shall not pervert justice. You shall not show partiality, and you shall not accept a bribe, for a bribe blinds the eyes of the wise and subverts the cause of the righteous. 20 Justice, and only justice, you shall follow, that you may live and inherit the land that the LORD your God is giving you." (Deuteronomy 16:19–20 ESV)

The proscription against bribery applies not only to those in authority but also to anyone who is offered a reward to perform an unjust act. Deuteronomy 27:25 specifically states, "Cursed be anyone who takes a bribe to shed innocent blood" (ESV).

However, if you avoid bribery and corruption and depend instead on God for your success, He will surely bless you. As David sang:

Blessed is the man
who walks not in the counsel of the wicked,
nor stands in the way of sinners,
nor sits in the seat of scoffers;

2 but his delight is in the law of the LORD,
and on his law he meditates day and night.
3 He is like a tree
planted by streams of water
that yields its fruit in its season
 and its leaf does not wither.
In all that he does, he prospers.
4 The wicked are not so,
but are like chaff that the wind drives away.
(Psalm 1:1–4 ESV)
The boastful shall not stand before your eyes;
you hate all evildoers.
6 You destroy those who speak lies;
the LORD abhors the bloodthirsty
and deceitful man. (Psalm 5:1–6 ESV)

CHAPTER THIRTEEN
ABRAHAM THE BELIEVER

*B*elief is central to success, as we learned in chapter 6 when we discussed the law of believing. Remember that the greatest blessings of Abraham's success stage in life began when he parted ways from his nephew Lot (Genesis 13:14–16). As Abraham removed himself from the hindering influence of Lot, you too must identify and separate yourself from the unrighteous and unhelpful people, activities, and other elements of your life that stand in the way of God's intended blessings. Jesus Himself taught us this lesson when He cursed the fruitless fig tree (Matthew 21:18–19).

Many things in our lives are fruitless. They do not produce anything or add value to our daily lives, yet we persist in them. If you think that Jesus dealt harshly with the fig tree, then realize that you must also be uncompromising with the garbage in your life. Take time to assess your life carefully, honestly, even brutally, and you will see that you are wasting much of your time and energy in ways that do not align with your God-inspired goals or purposes.

THE CALL WITH PROMISE

Abraham was a forgiver; he was a giver; he was a man of justice and integrity; and he was extremely wealthy. Without a doubt, Abraham was morally upright and materially rich. However, none of these qualities made Abraham a believer. In your spiritual journey, you must understand that leading a generally morally life and amassing earthly riches cannot make you wholly righteous and achieve the ultimate rewards. Writing to the Ephesians, Paul explained the additional, key variable that is necessary if you want to experience spiritual prosperity in full:

> At one time you were like a dead person because of the things you did wrong and your offenses against God. 2 You used to live like people of this world. You followed the rule of a destructive spiritual power. This is the spirit of disobedience to God's will that is now at work in persons whose lives are characterized by disobedience. 3 At one time you were like those persons. All of you used to do whatever felt good and whatever you thought you wanted so that you were children headed for punishment just like everyone else.
> 4–5 However, God is rich in mercy. He brought us to life in Christ while we were dead as a result of those things we did wrong. He did this because of the great love that he has for us. 6 And God raised us up and seated us in the heavens with Christ Jesus. 7 God did this to show future generations the greatness of his grace by the goodness that God has shown us in Christ Jesus.
> 8 You are saved by God's grace because of your faith. This salvation is God's gift. It's not something you possessed. 9 It's not something you did that you can be proud of. 10 Instead, we are God's accomplishment, created in Christ Jesus to do good things. God planned for these good things to be the way that we live our lives. (Ephesians 2:1–10 CEB)

When someone in our society becomes rich and famous, that person becomes a god to his or her followers. The person comes to believe in himself or herself instead of in God. However, Abraham remembered that God was ultimately responsible for liberating him from the false religions of Ur and bringing him every kind of success, despite his unworthiness. Therefore, Abraham "believed the LORD," who "counted it to him as righteousness" (Genesis 15:6 ESV); and his material prosperity only grew as a result of his unlimited spiritual credit with God.

Abraham's children in faith (Galatians 3:7) receive the same good credit. In discussing Abraham, James 2:22–23 explains that faith allows us to be friends to God:

See, his faith was at work along with his actions. In fact, his faith was made complete by his faithful actions. 23 So the scripture was fulfilled that says, Abraham believed God, and God regarded him as righteous. What is more, Abraham was called God's friend. (CEB, emphasis in original)

Life Application #8

Most teachings about salvation are false. The Bible establishes without a doubt that there is only one way to heaven—Jesus Christ. As the saying goes, attending church every Sunday doesn't make someone a Christian any more than eating at McDonald's makes a person a hamburger. Contrary to the way in which most people in the world view religion, you aren't truly a Christian simply because your parents were Christians or baptized you as a child. Christianity is not even a religion, in terms of being based on rituals, but a set of relationships—a vertical relationship with God and horizontal relationships with our neighbors, all made possible by our acceptance of Jesus Christ. Thus, Christianity begins with a personal decision that no one else can make for you.

Abraham's relatives were pagan worshipers, according to Joshua 24:2. Although Abraham could easily have remained in the false religion of his family, he reached a point in his life when he knew that he needed to believe in God alone. Abraham realized that neither his old life nor the money and fame that he eventually attained could secure him in righteousness and success. Therefore, he devoted his life to God in order to enjoy all that God had given him and planned for him. Rich and famous people often face challenges and struggles, and end up destroying themselves, because there is something missing in their lives that no amount of money, drugs, or human adoration can provide.

Abraham realized that he needed spiritual food, which is the word of God. Most people starve their spirits and leave their souls malnourished because they only gratify their bodies, feeding the soul with the wrong sorts of people and neglecting the spirit completely. As Jesus said, "Man shall not live on bread alone, but on every word that comes from the mouth of God" (Matthew 4:4 NIV).

Corollary to the Law of Believing

The law of believing—"If you believe, it will work"—thus requires a follow-up rule to address the question, "Then in whom or what should I believe?" Though many religions claim to be the best, Abraham did not believe in any particular religion or religious leader. He did, however, believe in God, and this relationship led him to spiritual freedom and all manner of success. Do not let the claims of particular leaders or denominations confuse you or derail your focus from

God and His word. The corollary to the law of believing, then, is this: Believe in Jesus Christ as the Way to a personal relationship with God.

There are no religions or denominations in heaven, and God judges us based on our actions and hearts while we are here on earth. It is important for you to focus on God and Jesus because they are the source and the completion of the faith that guides us to live successfully. Jesus is God, but He came to earth to show us how we should live. He experienced everything that we endure in our lives today. He cried; He grew angry; He became hungry; He prayed; He died.

The following scriptures describe Jesus as both God and, at the same time, the Son of God:

> In the beginning was the Word, and the Word was with God, and the Word was God. 2 He was with God in the beginning. 3 Through him all things were made; without him nothing was made that has been made. 4 In him was life, and that life was the light of all mankind. ... 14 The Word became flesh and made his dwelling among us. We have seen his glory, the glory of the one and only Son, who came from the Father, full of grace and truth. (John 1:1–4, 14 NIV)

"The LORD possessed [or fathered] me at the beginning of his work,
the first of his acts of old.
23 Ages ago I was set up,
at the first, before the beginning of the earth. ...
30 then I was beside him, like a master workman,
and I was daily his delight,
rejoicing before him always,
31 rejoicing in his inhabited world

and delighting in the children of man.
32 "And now, O sons, listen to me:
blessed are those who keep my ways.
33 Hear instruction and be wise,
do not neglect it.
34 Blessed is the one who listens to me,
watching daily at my gates,
waiting beside my doors.
35 For whoever finds me finds life
and obtains favor from the LORD,
36 but he who who fails to find me injures himself;
all who hate me love death." (Proverbs 8:22–23, 30–36 ESV)

Whom you believe and what you believe as guides for your spiritual journey are of utmost importance if you want to build wealth here on earth and in heaven. Your spiritual life should be of paramount concern, in part because it allows you to attain the inner peace that will permit you to enjoy the rest of God's blessings in this life.

The purpose of Jesus' life was for Him to become the Savior of all people; this is why He was born (Luke 2:10–11). For Jesus to be your Savior, you must treat His love as your most precious possession. Here is how I treat a gift I love: (1) I think about that gift; (2) I talk about that gift; and (3) I use that gift. To ensure that you hold your relationship with Jesus in the same regard, you must practice the following three aspects of the corollary to the law of believing:

1. Believe Jesus as your Savior.

Those who claim that Jesus was only a human teacher should take heed of Christ's own words on the matter:

"Do not let your hearts be troubled. You believe in God; believe also in me. 2 My Father's house has many rooms; if that were not so, would I have told you that I am going there to prepare a place for you? 3 And if I go and prepare a place for you, I will come back and take you to be with me that you also may be where I am." ... 6 Jesus answered, "I am the way and the truth and the life. No one comes to the Father except through me." (John 14:1–3, 6 NIV)

For God so loved the world that he gave his one and only Son, that whoever believes in him shall not perish but have eternal life. 17 For God did not send his Son into the world to condemn the world, but to save the world through him. 18 Whoever believes in him is not condemned, but whoever does not believe stands condemned already because they have not believed in the name of God's one and only Son. (John 3:16–18 NIV)

"He who believes in the Son has eternal life; but he who does not obey the Son will not see life, but the wrath of God abides on him." (John 3:36 NASB)

2. Talk about Jesus.

The law of believing requires that you say what you believe; likewise, the corollary requires you to confess that Jesus is your risen Lord and Savior (Roman 10:9–10). Jesus wants us to talk about Him to those who haven't heard about Him. We believers must show our appreciation by letting others know what He is doing in our lives. To shy from doing so proves a weakness of belief and lack of commitment that endanger your spiritual life, as Jesus Himself explained:

"For whoever is ashamed of me and of my words in this adulterous and sinful generation, of him will the Son of Man also be ashamed when he comes in the glory of his Father with the holy angels." (Mark 8:38 ESV)

"Whoever acknowledges me before others, I will also acknowledge before my Father in heaven. 33 But whoever disowns me before others, I will disown before my Father in heaven." (Matthew 10: 32–33 NIV)

3. Use Jesus in your life.

Better than anyone else, Jesus knows everything that we are going through in our lives. Not only did He experience life on earth in person but He also died for every wrongdoing that we commit in our lives today. He did this so that we could have the best possible relationship with God, and we must use His gift instead of taking His sacrifice for granted. The prophet Isaiah tells us what Jesus endured because of our sins:

> He was despised and rejected by men;
> a man of sorrows, and acquainted with grief;
> and as one from whom men hide their faces
> he was despised, and we esteemed him not.
> 4 Surely he has borne our griefs
> and carried our sorrows;
> yet we esteemed him stricken,
> smitten by God, and afflicted.
> 5 But he was pierced for our transgressions;
> he was crushed for our iniquities;
> upon him was the chastisement that brought us peace,
> and with his wounds we are healed.
> 6 All we like sheep have gone astray;
> we have turned — every one — to his own way;

and the LORD has laid on him
the iniquity of us all. ...
9 And they made his grave with the wicked,
and with a rich man in his death,
although he had done no violence,
and there was no deceit in his mouth.
10 Yet it was the will of the LORD to crush him;
he has put him to grief;
when his soul makes an offering for guilt,
he shall see his offspring; he shall prolong his days,
the will of the LORD shall prosper in his hand.
11 Out of the anguish of his soul he shall see and be satisfied;
by his knowledge shall the righteous one, my servant,
make many to be accounted righteous,
and he shall bear their iniquities.
12 Therefore I will divide him a portion with
the many [or the great],
and he shall divide the spoil with the strong,
because he poured out his soul to death
and was numbered with the transgressors;
yet he bore the sin of many,
and makes intercession for the transgressors.
(Isaiah 53:3–6, 9–12 ESV)

Thus, Jesus suffered grievously on our behalf. He also performed numerous miracles that no man could duplicate, thereby proving that He was who He said He was:

Jesus Changes Water into Wine

On the third day a wedding took place at Cana in Galilee. Jesus' mother was there, 2 and Jesus and his disciples had also been invited to the wedding. 3 When the wine was gone, Jesus' mother said to him, they have no more wine.

THE CALL WITH PROMISE

4 "Woman why do you involve me?" Jesus replied. "My hour has not yet come.
5 His mother said to the servants, "Do whatever he tells you."
6 Nearby stood six stone water jars, the kind used by the Jews for ceremonial washing, each holding from twenty to thirty gallons.
7 Jesus said to the servants, "Fill the jars with water"; so they filled them to the brim.
8 Then he told them, "Now draw some out and take it to the master of the banquet."
They did so, 9 and the master of the banquet tasted the water that had been turned into wine. He did not realize where it had come from, though the servants who had drawn the water knew. Then he called the bridegroom aside 10 and said, "Everyone brings out the choice wine first and then the cheaper wine after the guests have had too much to drink; but you have saved the best till now."
11 What Jesus did here in Cana of Galilee was the first of the signs through which he revealed his glory; and his disciples believed in him. (John 2:1–11 NIV)

The First Miraculous Catch of Fish

When he had finished speaking, he said to Simon, "Put out into deep water, and let down the nets for a catch.
5 Simon answered, "Master, we've worked hard all night and haven't caught anything. But because you say so, I will let down the nets."
6 When they had done so, they caught such a large number of fish that their nets began to break. 7 So they signaled their partners in the other boat to come and help them, and they came and filled both boats so full that they began to sink.
8 When Simon Peter saw this, he fell at Jesus' knees and said, "Go away from me, Lord; I am a sinful man!" 9 For he

and all his companions were astonished at the catch of fish they had taken, 10 and so were James and John, the sons of Zebedee, Simon's partners.
Then Jesus said to Simon, "Don't be afraid; from now on you will fish for people." (Luke 5:4–10 NIV)

Jesus Calms the Storm

Then he got into the boat and his disciples followed him. 24 Suddenly a furious storm came up on the lake, so that the waves swept over the boat. But Jesus was sleeping. 25 The disciples went and woke him, saying, and "Lord, save us we're going to drown!"
26 He replied, "You of little faith, why are you so afraid?" Then he got up and rebuked the winds and the waves, and it was completely calm.
27 The men were amazed and asked, "What kind of man is this? Even the winds and the waves obey him!"
(Matthew 8:23–27 NIV)

Jesus Feeds the Five Thousand

When Jesus heard what had happened he withdrew by boat privately to a solitary place. Hearing of this, the crowds followed him on foot from the towns. 14 When Jesus landed and saw a large crowd, he had compassion on them and healed their sick.
15 As evening approached, the disciples came to him and said, "This is a remote place, and it's already getting late. Send the crowds away, so they can go to the villages and buy themselves some food."
16 Jesus replied, "They do not need to go away. You give them something to eat.

THE CALL WITH PROMISE

17 "We have here only five loaves of bread and two fish," they answered.
18 "Bring them here to me," he said. 19 And he directed the people to sit down on the grass. Taking the five loaves and the two fish and looking up to heaven, he gave thanks and broke the loaves. Then he gave them to the disciples, and the disciples gave them to the people. 20 They all ate and were satisfied, and the disciples picked up twelve basketfuls of broken pieces that were left over. 21 The number of those who ate was about five thousand men, besides women and children. (Matthew 14:13–21 NIV)

Jesus Walks on the Water

Immediately Jesus made the disciples get into the boat and go on ahead of him to the other side, while he dismissed the crowd. 23 After he had dismissed them, he went up on a mountainside by himself to pray. Later that night, he was there alone, 24 but the boat was already a considerable distance from land, buffeted by the waves because the wind was against it.
25 Shortly before dawn Jesus went out to them, walking on the lake. 26 When the disciples saw him walking on the lake, they were terrified. "It's a ghost," they said, and cried out in fear.
27 But Jesus immediately said to them: "Take courage! It is I. don't be afraid."
28 "Lord, if it's you," Peter replied, "tell me to come to you on the water."
29 "Come," he said.
Then Peter got down out of the boat, walked on the water and came toward Jesus. 30 But when he saw the wind, he was afraid and, beginning to sink, cried out, "Lord, save me!"

31 Immediately Jesus reached out his hand and caught him. You of little faith, he said, why did you doubt?"
32 And when they climbed into the boat, the wind died down. 33 Then those who were in the boat worshiped him, saying, "Truly you are the Son of God." (Matthew 14:22–33 NIV)

Though Abraham was rich by earthly standards, he believed and trusted in God because he knew that worldly riches do not last. If we believe in God, we will live forever, for Jesus is the food that sustains our spirits eternally:

When they found him on the other side of the lake, they asked him, "Rabbi, when did you get here?"
26 Jesus answered, "Very truly I tell you, you are looking for me, not because you saw the signs I performed but because you ate the loaves and had your fill. 27 Do not work for food that spoils, but for food that endures to eternal life, which the Son of Man will give you. For on him God the Father has placed his seal of approval."
28 Then they asked him, "What must we do to do the works God requires?"
29 Jesus answered, "The work of God is this: to believe in the one he has sent."
30 So they asked him, "What sign then will you give that we may see it and believe you? What will you do? 31 Our ancestors ate the manna in the wilderness; as it is written: 'He gave them bread from heaven to eat.'"
32 Jesus said to them, "Very truly I tell you, it is not Moses who has given you the bread from heaven, but it is my Father who gives you the true bread from heaven. 33 For the bread of God is the bread that comes down from heaven and gives life to the world."
34 "Sir," they said, "always give us this bread."

35 Then Jesus declared, "I am the bread of life. Whoever comes to me will never go hungry, and whoever believes in me will never be thirsty. 36 But as I told you, you have seen me and still you do not believe. 37 All those the Father gives me will come to me, and whoever comes to me I will never drive away. 38 For I have come down from heaven not to do my will but to do the will of him who sent me. 39 And this is the will of him who sent me that I shall lose none of all those he has given me, but raise them up at the last day. 40 For my Father's will is that everyone who looks to the Son and believes in him shall have eternal life, and I will raise them up at the last day." (John 6:25–40 NIV)

Jesus can accomplish anything on our behalf; after all, he even brought the dead to life (John 11) and secured everlasting life for all believers. He knows how to solve your everyday challenges, both great and small, as well. Like the blind beggar, simply tell the Lord your problems:

As Jesus approached Jericho; a blind man was sitting by the roadside begging. 36 When he heard the crowd going by, he asked what was happening. 37 They told him, "Jesus of Nazareth is passing by."
38 He called out, "Jesus, Son of David, have mercy on me!"
39 Those who led the way rebuked him and told him to be quiet, but he shouted all the more, "Son of David, have mercy on me!"
40 Jesus stopped and ordered the man to be brought to him. When he came near, Jesus asked him, 41 "What do you want me to do for you?"
"Lord, I want to see," he replied.
42 Jesus said to him, "Receive your sight; your faith has healed you." 43 Immediately he received his sight and followed Jesus, praising God. (Luke 18:35–43 NIV)

How is your relationship with God? If we want the best, we have to build a strong relationship with God. He will never leave you nor forsake you. With God, you are very sure of your life. Perhaps you live in fear and uncerterntity. Trust God fully and don't doubt who God is, but trust what He can do for you.

CHAPTER FOURTEEN

ABRAHAM's TRIALS AND BLESSINGS

When you give your life to Christ, you may assume that everything should flow smoothly from then on. However, God often allows us to be tested so that our belief is strengthened. As a result, life becomes a blend of different tastes—sweet, bitter, and sour. If we ate the exact same food every day, no matter how good it tasted, we would become bored. Thankfully, as a believer, you can expect variety in life.

Human beings long for life to be smooth and comfortable. Any time when we face problems in our workplace, health, or relationships, we tend to complain. Problems, though, are inevitable in this life; so when you face any challenge, remember that belief in God will always enable you to overcome that situation. Moreover, as the book of James reassures us, trials bring us spiritual blessings:

Count it all joy, my brothers, when you meet trials of various kinds, 3 for you know that the testing of your faith produces steadfastness. 4 And let steadfastness have its full effect, that you may be perfect and complete, lacking in nothing.
5 If any of you lacks wisdom, let him ask God, who gives generously to all without reproach, and it will be given him. 6 But let him ask in faith, without doubting, for the one who doubts is like a wave of the sea that is driven and tossed by the wind. 7 For that person must not suppose that he will receive anything from the Lord; 8 he is a double-minded man, unstable in all his ways.
9 Let the lowly brother boast in his exaltation, 10 and the rich in his humiliation, because like a flower of the grass he will pass away. 11 For the sun rises with its scorching heat and withers the grass; its flower falls, and its beauty perishes. So also will the rich man fade away in the midst of his pursuits.
12 Blessed is the man who remains steadfast under trial, for when he has stood the test he will receive the crown of life, which God has promised to those who love him. 13 Let no one say when he is tempted, "I am being tempted by God," for God cannot be tempted with evil, and he himself tempts no one. 14 But each person is tempted when he is lured and enticed by his own desire. 15 Then desire when it has conceived gives birth to sin, and sin when it is fully grown brings forth death.
16 Do not be deceived, my beloved brothers. 17 Every good and every perfect gift is from above, coming down from the Father of lights with whom there is no variation or shadow due to change. 18 Of his own will he brought us forth by the word of truth, that we should be a kind of firstfruits of his creatures. (James 1:2–18 ESV)

Life Applications #9

Sometimes we feel as if God must practice favoritism or selective hearing because He answers some prayers but rejects others. The truth, however, is that God responds to prayers in the way and timing that He knows to be in our ultimate best interest. If you ask for something in prayer but pray based on your own will and understanding, imperfectly aligned with His, then He may not answer your prayer immediately or as you expect. Does a loving parent surrender to every demand a child makes? The closer you become to God through your relationship with Jesus, the more often you and God will be on the same page, as Abraham was. As James explained, "Draw near to God, and he will draw near to you. Cleanse your hands, you sinners, and purify your hearts, you double-minded" (James 4:8 ESV).

Abraham, too, experienced sweet, bitter, and sour times. When God revealed to him, in a dream, some of the hardships and blessings that he and his people would experience, the effect must have been bittersweet for Abraham:

> As the sun was setting, Abram fell into a deep sleep, and a thick and dreadful darkness came over him. 13 Then the LORD said to him, "Know for certain that for four hundred years your descendants will be strangers in a country not their own and that they will be enslaved and mistreated there. 14 But I will punish the nation they serve as slaves, and afterward they will come out with great possessions. 15 You however, will go to your ancestors in peace and be buried at a good old age...."
> 17 When the sun had set and darkness had fallen, a smoking firepot with a blazing torch appeared and passed between the pieces. 18 On that day the LORD made a covenant with Abram and said, "To your descendants I give this land, from

the Wadi of Egypt to the great river, the Euphrates— 19 the land of the Kenites, Kenizzites, Kadmonites, 20 Hittites, Perizzites, Rephaites, 21 Amorites, Canaanites, Girgashites and Jebusites." (Genesis 15:12-15, 17-21 NIV)

When Abraham's fear led him to deceive Abimelek, one of his hosts, into thinking that Sarah was not his wife—and Abimelek then decided to take Sarah for himself—God did not abandon Abraham but instead transformed a bitter situation into one of unexpected blessing:

Now Abraham moved on from there into the region of the Negev and lived between Kadesh and Shur. For a while he stayed in Gerar, 2 and there Abraham said of his wife Sarah, "She is my sister." Then Abimelek king of Gerar sent for Sarah and took her.
3 But God came to Abimelech in a dream one night and said to him, "You are as good as dead because of the woman you have taken; she is a married woman."
4 Now Abimelek had not gone near her, so he said, "Lord, will you destroy an innocent nation? 5 Did he not say to me, 'She is my sister,' and didn't she also say, 'He is my brother'? I have done this with a clear conscience and clean hands."
6 Then God said to him in the dream, "Yes, I know you did this with a clear conscience, and so I have kept you from sinning against me. That is why I did not let you touch her. 7 Now return the man's wife, for he is a prophet, and he will pray for you and you will live. But if you do not return her, you may be sure that you and all who belong to you will die."
8 Early the next morning Abimelek summoned all his officials, and when he told them all that had happened, they were very much afraid. 9 Then Abimelek called Abraham in and said, "What have you done to us? How have I wronged you that you have brought such great guilt upon me and my

kingdom? You have done things to me that should never be done." 10 And Abimelek asked Abraham, "What was your reason for doing this?"

11 Abraham replied, "I said to myself, 'There is surely no fear of God in this place, and they will kill me because of my wife.' 12 Besides, she really is my sister, the daughter of my father though not of my mother; and she became my wife. 13 And when God had me wander from my father's household, I said to her, 'This is how you can show your love to me: Everywhere we go, say of me, "He is my brother."'"

14 Then Abimelek brought sheep and cattle and male and female slaves and gave them to Abraham, and he returned Sarah his wife to him. 15 And Abimelek said, "My land is before you; live wherever you like."

16 To Sarah he said, "I am giving your brother a thousand shekels of silver. This is to cover the offense against you before all who are with you; you are completely vindicated."

17 Then Abraham prayed to God, and God healed Abimelek, his wife and his female slaves so they could have children again.... (Genesis 20:1–17 NIV)

Abraham was afraid that they would kill him because of his wife. However, God protected him without even giving Abraham advance notice. Faith in God through Christ will protect you, too; and Jesus said of his followers that "they will pick up snakes with their hands; and when they drink deadly poison, it will not hurt them at all; they will place their hands on sick people, and they will get well" (Mark 16:18 NIV). On another occasion, Jesus declared, "Behold, I have given you power to tread on serpents and scorpions, and over all the power of the enemy, and nothing shall hurt you" (Luke 10:19 ESV).

This does not mean that you should test God by drinking poison or walking on snakes. If, on the other hand, you have

ABRAHAM's TRIALS AND BLESSINGS

already made a misstep or committed a wrong, as Abraham did when he said that Sarah was only his "sister" (cousin), then God will rescue you. In our lives, we sometimes make mistakes so terrible that we think the only possible result must be death, as if we truly had drunk poison. When your situation seems hopeless, do not give up; rather, continue to believe that God can make a way where none seems to exist. God can turn poison to praise if you believe that He will.

Abraham knew that he couldn't fight Abimalek or the other powerful men of Gerar if they decided to take Sarah from him. As God eventually reminded Abraham, however, he did not need to rely on his own strength. God is ready to be the champion and protector of those who approach Him. No matter what the enemy has taken from you, if you believe in Jesus as your Savior, you will find yourself blessed.

Twenty-five years after Abraham and his wife left their home in Ur, God appeared to Abraham with the sweetest news of all. Though Abraham was nearly a century old and his wife was ninety years old, God repeated His earlier promises and revealed that He would bless them with a son:

> When Abram was ninety-nine years old, the LORD appeared to him and said, "I am God Almighty; walk before me faithfully and be blameless. 2 I will confirm my covenant between me and you and will greatly increase your numbers."
> 3 Abram fell facedown, and God said to him, 4 "As for me, this is my covenant with you: You will be the father of many nations. 5 No longer will you be called Abram your name will be Abraham, for I have made you a father of many nations. 6 I will make you very fruitful; I will make nations of you, and kings will come from you. 7 I will establish my covenant as an everlasting covenant between me and you

THE CALL WITH PROMISE

and your descendants after you for the generations to come, to be your God and the God of your descendants after you. 8 The whole land of Canaan, where you now reside as a foreigner, I will give as an everlasting possession to you and your descendants after you; and I will be their God."

9 Then God said to Abraham, "As for you, you must keep my covenant, you and your descendants after you for the generations to come. 10 This is my covenant with you and your descendants after you, the covenant you are to keep: Every male among you shall be circumcised. 11 You are to undergo circumcision, and it will be the sign of the covenant between me and you. 12 For the generations to come every male among you who is eight days old must be circumcised, including those born in your household or bought with money from a foreigner—those who are not your offspring. 13 Whether born in your household or bought with your money, they must be circumcised. My covenant in your flesh is to be an everlasting covenant. 14 Any uncircumcised male, who has not been circumcised in the flesh, will be cut off from his people; he has broken my covenant."

15 God also said to Abraham, "As for Sarai your wife, you are no longer to call her Sarai; her name will be Sarah. I will bless her and will surely give you a son by her. 16 I will bless her so that she will be the mother of nations; kings of peoples will come from her."

17 Abraham fell facedown; he laughed and said to himself, "Will a son be born to a man a hundred years old? Will Sarah bear a child at the age of ninety?" 18 And Abraham said to God, "If only Ishmael might live under your blessing!"

19 Then God said, "Yes, but your wife Sarah will bear you a son, and you will call him Isaac. I will establish my covenant with him as an everlasting covenant for his descendants after him. 20 And as for Ishmael, I have heard you: I will surely bless him; I will make him fruitful and

will greatly increase his numbers. He will be the father of twelve rulers, and I will make him into a great nation. 21 But my covenant I will establish with Isaac, whom Sarah will bear to you by this time next year." 22 When he had finished speaking with Abraham, God went up from him. (Genesis 17:1–22 NIV)

Note that God changed Abram's name ("high father") to Abraham ("father of many") in Genesis 17:5 and Sarai's name ("my princess") to Sarah ("mother of nations") in Genesis 17:15. Below are some prominent examples of other biblical figures who changed their names, often at God's direct prompting:

- Jacob ("supplanter") was changed to Israel ("he who has the power of God") (Genesis 32:28).
- Simon ("God has heard") was changed to Peter ("Rock") (John 1:42).
- Naomi ("beautiful") was changed to Mara ("bitter") (Ruth 1:20).
- Saul was changed to Paul (Acts 13:9).
- Joseph was changed to Zaphenath-Paneah (Genesis 41:45).
- Daniel was changed to Belteshazzar (Daniel 1:7).
- Hadassah was changed to Esther ("star") (Esther 2:7).
- Solomon was changed to Jedidiah (2 Samuel 12:24).

Does a change of name have any spiritual significance? The Bible does not directly explain the importance of changing names. Some cultures and countries believe that names have an influence over children's personalities and lives. Along similar lines, people in ancient times associated names with identity, and the act of naming someone was a demonstration of authority. In the Bible, people usually change their names after experiencing an ordeal or encounter that transforms their circumstances, their relationship with God, or some other aspect of their identity.

Likewise, the Bible reveals that there will one day be a name change for all believers as a result of our salvation through Christ: "If you can hear, listen to what the Spirit is saying to the churches: I will give those who emerge victorious some of the hidden manna to eat. I will also give to each of them a white stone with a new name written on it, which no one knows except the one who receives it" (Revelation 2:17 CEB).

God marked Abraham and Sarah as His by giving them new names; and, as promised, He blessed them with a son of their own, whom Abraham marked physically as God's through the rite of circumcision:

> Now the LORD was gracious to Sarah as he had said, and the LORD did for Sarah what he had promised. 2 Sarah became pregnant and bore a son to Abraham in his old age; at the very time God had promised him. 3 Abraham gave the name Isaac to the son Sarah bore him. 4 When his son Isaac was eight days old, Abraham circumcised him, as God commanded him. 5 Abraham was a hundred years old when his son Isaac was born to him.
> 6 Sarah said, "God has brought me laughter, and everyone who hears about this will laugh with me." 7 And she added, "Who would have said to Abraham that Sarah would nurse children? Yet I have borne him a son in his old age." (Genesis 21:1–7 NIV)

After twenty-five years, Abraham's prayers had finally been answered. Believers often find it difficult to wait for the right time—God's time. Sometimes we make hasty decisions because of our impatience or hopelessness. This is why Jesus had to remind His disciples, "With man this is impossible, but with God all things are possible" (Matthew 19:26 NIV). The words of Isaiah remind us that God lends His power and wisdom to those who are patient:

> Hast thou not known? hast thou not heard, that the everlasting God, the LORD, the Creator of the ends of the earth, fainteth not, neither is weary? there is no searching of his understanding.
> 29 He giveth power to the faint; and to them that have no might he increaseth strength.
> 30 Even the youths shall faint and be weary, and the young men shall utterly fall:
> 31 But they that wait upon the LORD shall renew their strength; they shall mount up with wings as eagles; they shall run, and not be weary; and they shall walk, and not faint. (Isaiah 40:28–31 KJV)

If you maintain your faith and trust in the Lord, He will work miracles for you. As long as there is breath left in you, you should remain in hope. The book of Ecclesiastes 9:4 observes, "But he who is joined with all the living has hope, for a living dog is better than a dead lion" (Ecclesiastes 9:4 ESV).

Abraham's life was not sweet every day, either, yet he did not give up on God. We must praise and thank God for everything, even amidst hardship. Let us turn our complaints to compliments, our problems to praises, our burden to blessings, and our fear and feelings to faith. Through our relationship with Jesus, we are overcomers no matter our circumstances. Abraham kept his faith and hope even when God asked the unthinkable of him—to sacrifice his beloved son:

> Some time later God tested Abraham. He said to him, "Abraham!"
> Here I am, he replied.

THE CALL WITH PROMISE

2 Then God said, "Take your son, your only son, whom you love— Isaac—and go to the region of Moriah. Sacrifice him there as a burnt offering on a mountain I will show you."
3 Early the next morning Abraham got up and loaded his donkey. He took with him two of his servants and his son Isaac. When he had cut enough wood for the burnt offering, he set out for the place God had told him about. 4 On the third day Abraham looked up and saw the place in the distance. 5 He said to his servants, "Stay here with the donkey while I and the boy go over there. We will worship and then we will come back to you."
6 Abraham took the wood for the burnt offering and placed it on his son Isaac, and he himself carried the fire and the knife. As the two of them went on together, 7 Isaac spoke up and said to his father Abraham, "Father?"
"Yes, my son?" Abraham replied.
"The fire and wood are here," Isaac said, "but where is the lamb for the burnt offering?"
8 Abraham answered, "God himself will provide the lamb for the burnt offering, my son." And the two of them went on together.
9 When they reached the place God had told him about, Abraham built an altar there and arranged the wood on it. He bound his son Isaac and laid him on the altar, on top of the wood. 10 Then he reached out his hand and took the knife to slay his son. 11 But the angel of the Lord called out to him from heaven, "Abraham! Abraham!"
"Here I am," he replied.
12 "Do not lay a hand on the boy," he said. "Do not do anything to him. Now I know that you fear God, because you have not withheld from me your son, your only son."
13 Abraham looked up and there in a thicket he saw a ram caught by its horns. He went over and took the ram and sacrificed it as a burnt offering instead of his son. 14 So Abraham called that place The LORD Will Provide. And

to this day it is said, "On the mountain of the LORD it will be provided."
15 The angel of the LORD called to Abraham from heaven a second time 16 and said, "I swear by myself, declares the LORD, that because you have done this and have not withheld your son, your only son, 17 I will surely bless you and make your descendants as numerous as the stars in the sky and as the sand on the seashore. Your descendants will take possession of the cities of their enemies, 18 and through your offspring all nations on earth will be blessed, because you have obeyed me." (Genesis 22:1–18 NIV)

Abraham was willing to offer Isaac, his and Sarah's only son, to God. Your "Isaac" is anything of great value that you could offer to the Lord. Perhaps your Isaac is your time and energy, which you could be offering to the church. Your Isaac might be the talents and resources that you could use to support works of ministry.

When you decide to offer your Isaac to God, avoid telling people who may discourage you. If Abraham had told his wife or servants that he was going to offer Isaac as a sacrifice to God, they would likely have tried to stop him. Oftentimes, when it comes to the work of God, those actions that will bring the greatest breakthroughs do not make sense to people around you. They will laugh at you and call you names; but you should know that God is watching and blessing is headed your way.

Abraham, like David, knew that a gift is valuable only if it represents a sacrifice on the giver's part. When David was offered the means to make a sacrifice to God, he answered, "'No, but I will buy it from you for a price. I will not offer burnt offerings to the LORD my God that cost me nothing" (2 Samuel 24:24 ESV).

We need to believe as Abraham believed in order to enjoy our spiritual journey with the Lord. God expects you to be like Abraham because otherwise, if your faith is unstable, you cause yourself more harm with every passing day. If you put your trust in God, He will never disappoint you. God will never break your heart, and He will always provide sheep to replace the Isaacs in your life. If you put your faith in God alone—in relationship, not religion—then you will live a successful, victorious life.

Jesus reminded us what Abraham knew—that even family is not as important as obedience in faith:

> "He who loves father or mother more than Me is not worthy of Me; and he who loves son or daughter more than Me is not worthy of Me. 38 And he who does not take his cross and follow after Me is not worthy of Me." (Matthew 10:37–38 NKJV)

God deserves the best of everything we have, including our time, energy, and resources. Paul instructed the Corinthians, "So, whether you eat or drink or whatever you do, you should do it all for God's glory" (1 Corinthians 10:31 CEB).

This is not to say that family is unimportant. To the contrary, Abraham valued his family more highly than he did anything or anyone but God, and he repeatedly demonstrated his belief in God in his actions toward his family.

For instance, in ancient times, wealthy men were expected to acquire many wives; yet Abraham did not do so. Yes, Abraham practiced polygamy to the extent of taking several concubines, but clearly he loved and esteemed Sarah as his one and only true wife for as long as she lived. He understood that a man is supposed to "hold fast to his wife" (Genesis 2:24

ESV). Even today, men who become as rich and successful as Abraham often choose to celebrate their success with many different women. Some will even drive away their first wife, who likely supported them through many trials on the road to prosperity.

The New Testament specifically establishes monogamy as one of the key qualifications for model believers, especially those who wish to become spiritual leaders:

> The saying is trustworthy: If anyone aspires to the office of overseer, he desires a noble task. 2 Therefore an overseer must be above reproach, the husband of one wife, sober-minded, self-controlled, respectable, hospitable, able to teach, 3 not a drunkard, not violent but gentle, not quarrelsome, not a lover of money. 4 He must manage his own household well, with all dignity keeping his children submissive, 5 for if someone does not know how to manage his own household, how will he care for God's church? (1 Timothy 3:1–5 ESV)

Similarly, the book of Titus describes a "blameless" man as one who is "the husband of one wife, and his children are believers and not open to the charge of debauchery or insubordination" (Titus 1:6 ESV).

Abraham had chosen wisely in Sarah, a woman who shared his faith in God. As the adage goes, there is a woman behind every successful man; and, by the same token, a woman can be man's downfall—though not without his cooperation, mind you. Samson and Delilah offer one example of the latter (Judges 16), and King Solomon, the richest and most powerful of Israel's earthly kings, offers another:

THE CALL WITH PROMISE

> He [Solomon] had 700 wives, who were princesses, and 300 concubines. And his wives turned away his heart. 4 For when Solomon was old his wives turned away his heart after other gods, and his heart was not wholly true to the LORD his God, as was the heart of David his father. (1 Kings 11:3–4 ESV)

Abraham respected his wife Sarah all their lives. Even when Abraham took her servant Hagar to try to produce a child, he did so at Sarah's suggestion:

> Now Sarai, Abram's wife, had borne him no children. But she had an Egyptian slave named Hagar; 2 so she said to Abram, "The LORD has kept me from having children. Go, sleep with my slave; perhaps I can build a family through her."
> Abram agreed to what Sarai said. 3 So after Abram had been living in Canaan ten years, Sarai his wife took her Egyptian slave Hagar and gave her to her husband to be his wife. 4 He slept with Hagar, and she conceived. (Genesis 16:1–4 NIV)

Christians do not practice what Sarah did, and with good reason: Genesis 16:4 concludes, "When she [Hagar] knew she was pregnant, she began to despise her mistress" (NIV). Abraham and Sarah briefly let worry and hopelessness overtake them instead of remembering that children are a gift from God. You must wait upon the Lord, and God will bless you at the right time. If you and your spouse wish for children but are unable to have them, then God may intend for you to adopt one of the many children who are looking for parents.

More so than the production of babies, Christians today marry for friendship and companionship. Abraham and wife always seemed to be on the same page; in general, they communicated with one another and understood one another, and that is how a Christian home should be. Ephesians 5:22–33 addresses the relationship between husbands and wives, emphasizing the key importance of love and respect:

> For example, wives should submit to their husbands as if to the Lord. 23 A husband is the head of his wife like Christ is head of the church, that is, the savior of the body. 24 So wives submit to their husbands in everything as the church submits to Christ. 25 As for husbands, love your wives just like Christ loved the church and gave himself for her. 26 He did this to make her holy by washing her in a bath of water with the word. 27 He did this to present himself with a splendid church, one without any sort of stain or wrinkle on her clothes, but rather one that is holy and blameless. 28 That's how husbands ought to love their wives—in the same way as they do their own bodies. Anyone who loves his wife loves himself. 29 No one ever hates his own body, but feeds it and takes care of it just like Christ does for the church 30 because we are parts of his body. 31 This is why a man will leave his father and mother and be united with his wife, and the two of them will be one body. 32 Marriage is a significant allegory, and I'm applying it to Christ and the church. 33 In any case, as for you individually, each one of you should love his wife as himself, and wives should respect their husbands. (Ephesians 5:22–33 CEB, emphasis in original)

The book of 1 Peter adds, "Husbands, likewise, submit by living with your wife in ways that honor her, knowing that she is the weaker partner. Honor her all the more, as she is also a coheir of the gracious care [gift] of life. Do this so that your prayers won't be hindered" (1 Peter 3:7 CEB).

THE CALL WITH PROMISE

Though Paul described respect as properly a woman's attitude toward her husband, Abraham and Sarah demonstrated the mutuality of love and respect in marriage. Even when she died, Abraham continued to treat his wife with the utmost respect and consideration:

> Sarah lived to be a hundred and twenty-seven years old. 2 She died at Kiriath Arba (that is, Hebron) in the land of Canaan, and Abraham went to mourn for Sarah and to weep over her.
> 3 Then Abraham rose from beside his dead wife and spoke to the Hittites. He said, 4 "I am a foreigner and stranger among you. Sell me some property for a burial site here so I can bury my dead."
> 5 The Hittites replied to Abraham, 6 "Sir, listen to us. You are a mighty prince among us. Bury your dead in the choicest of our tombs. None of us will refuse you his tomb for burying your dead."
> 7 Then Abraham rose and bowed down before the people of the land, the Hittites. 8 He said to them, "If you are willing to let me bury my dead, then listen to me and intercede with Ephron son of Zohar on my behalf 9 so he will sell me the cave of Machpelah, which belongs to him and is at the end of his field. Ask him to sell it to me for the full price as a burial site among you."
> 10 Ephron the Hittite was sitting among his people and he replied to Abraham in the hearing of all the Hittites who had come to the gate of his city. 11 "No, my lord," he said. "Listen to me; I give you the field, and I give you the cave that is in it. I give it to you in the presence of my people. Bury your dead."
> 12 Again Abraham bowed down before the people of the land 13 and he said to Ephron in their hearing, "Listen to me, if you will. I will pay the price of the field. Accept it from me so I can bury my dead there."

14 Ephron answered Abraham, 15 "Listen to me, my lord; the land is worth four hundred shekels of silver, but what is that between you and me? Bury your dead."
16 Abraham agreed to Ephron's terms and weighed out for him the price he had named in the hearing of the Hittites: four hundred shekels of silver, according to the weight current among the merchants. (Genesis 23:1–16 NIV)

To honor his wife, Abraham humbled himself and asked permission from a man of lower status to buy Sarah's burial plot. By this time, Abraham was a prominent chief or lord, well known and powerful in the region. Nonetheless, he refused to take advantage of his neighbors. In the passage above, therefore, Abraham demonstrated that he was a true family man, honoring both his wife and God.

After the death of Sarah, Abraham prepared to help his son Isaac choose a wife. In doing so, he set an example to all believers as to how they might find a suitable spouse for themselves or their children:

As the days went by and Abraham became older, the LORD blessed Abraham in every way. 2 Abraham said to the oldest servant of his household, who was in charge of everything he owned, "Put your hand under my thigh. 3 By the LORD, God of heaven and earth, give me your word that you won't choose a wife for my son from the Canaanite women among whom I live. 4 Go to my land and my family and find a wife for my son Isaac there."
5 The servant said to him, "What if the woman doesn't agree to come back with me to this land? Shouldn't I take your son back to the land you left?"
6 Abraham said to him, "Be sure you don't take my son back there. 7 The LORD, God of heaven—who took me from my father's household and from my family's land,

THE CALL WITH PROMISE

who spoke with me and who gave me his word, saying, 'I will give this land to your descendants'—he will send his messenger in front of you, and you will find a wife for my son there. 8 If the woman won't agree to come back with you, you will be free from this obligation to me. Only don't take my son back there." 9 So the servant put his hand under his master Abraham's thigh and gave him his word about this mission.

10 The servant took ten of his master's camels and all of his master's best provisions, set out, and traveled to Nahor's city in Aram-naharaim. 11 He had his camels kneel down outside the city at the well in the evening, when women come out to draw water. 12 He said, "LORD, God of my master Abraham, make something good happen for me today and be loyal to my master Abraham. 13 I will stand here by the spring while the daughters of the men of the city come out to draw water. 14 When I say to a young woman, 'Hand me your water jar so I can drink,' and she says to me, 'Drink, and I will give your camels water too,' may she be the one you've selected for your servant Isaac. In this way I will know that you've been loyal to my master." 15 Even before he finished speaking, Rebekah—daughter of Bethuel the son of Milcah wife of Nahor, Abraham's brother—was coming out with a water jar on her shoulder. 16 The young woman was very beautiful, old enough to be married, and hadn't known a man intimately. She went down to the spring, filled her water jar, and came back up. 17 The servant ran to meet her and said, "Give me a little sip of water from your jar."

18 She said, "Drink, sir." Then she quickly lowered the water jar with her hands and gave him some water to drink. 19 When she finished giving him a drink, she said, "I'll draw some water for your camels too, till they've had enough to drink." 20 She emptied her water jar quickly into the watering trough, ran to the well again to draw water,

and drew for all of the camels. 21 The man stood gazing at her, wondering silently if the LORD had made his trip successful or not.

22 As soon as the camels had finished drinking, the man took out a gold ring, weighing a half shekel, and two gold bracelets for her arms, weighing ten shekels. 23 He said, "Please tell me whose daughter you are. Is there room in your father's house for us to spend the night?"

24 She responded, "I'm the daughter of Bethuel, who is the son of Milkah and Nahor." 25 She continued, "We have plenty of straw and feed for the camels, and a place to spend the night."

26 The man bowed down and praised the LORD: 27 "Bless the LORD, God of my master Abraham, who hasn't given up his loyalty and his faithfulness to my master. The LORD has shown me the way to the household of my master's brother."

28 The young woman ran and told her mother's household everything that had happened. 29 Rebekah had a brother named Laban, and Laban ran to the man outside by the spring. 30 When he had seen the ring and the bracelets on his sister's arms, and when he had heard his sister Rebekah say, "This is what the man said to me," he went to the man, who was still standing by the spring with his camels. 31 Laban said, "Come in, favored one of the LORD! Why are you standing outside? I've prepared the house and a place for the camels." 32 So the man entered the house. Then Laban unbridled the camels, provided straw and feed for them and water to wash his feet and the feet of the men with him, 33 and set out a meal for him.

But the man said, "I won't eat until I've said something." Laban replied, "Say it."

34 The man said, "I am Abraham's servant. 35 The LORD has richly blessed my master, has made him a great man, and has given him flocks, cattle, silver, gold, men servants,

women servants, camels, and donkeys. 36 My master's wife Sarah gave birth to a son for my master in her old age, and he's given him everything he owns. (Genesis 24:1–36 CEB)

The servant recounted the story of his mission for Abraham, then continued:

Laban and Bethuel both responded, "This is all the LORD's doing. We have nothing to say about it. 51 Here is Rebekah, right in front of you. Take her and go. She will be the wife of your master's son, just as the LORD said." 52 When Abraham's servant heard what they said, he bowed low before the LORD. 53 The servant brought out gold and silver jewelry and clothing and gave them to Rebekah. To her brother and to her mother he gave the finest gifts. 54 He and the men with him ate and drank and spent the night. When they got up in the morning, the servant said, "See me off to my master."
55 Her brother and mother said, "Let the young woman stay with us not more than ten days, and after that she may go." 56 But he said to them, "Don't delay me. The LORD has made my trip successful. See me off so that I can go to my master."
57 They said, "Summon the young woman and let's ask her opinion." 58 They called Rebekah and said to her, "Will you go with this man?"
She said, "I will go."
59 So they sent off their sister Rebekah, her nurse, Abraham's servant, and his men. 60 And they blessed Rebekah, saying to her,
"May you, our sister, may you become
thousands of ten thousand;
may your children possess
their enemies' cities."

61 Rebekah and her young women got up, mounted the camels, and followed the man. So the servant took Rebekah and left.
62 Now Isaac had come from the region of Beer-lahai-roi and had settled in the arid southern plain. 63 One evening, Isaac went out to inspect the pasture, and while staring he saw camels approaching. 64 Rebekah stared at Isaac. She got down from the camel 65 and said to the servant, "Who is this man walking through the pasture to meet us?"
The servant said, "He's my master." So she took her headscarf and covered herself. 66 The servant told Isaac everything that had happened. 67 Isaac brought Rebekah into his mother Sarah's tent. He received Rebekah as his wife and loved her. So Isaac found comfort after his mother's death. (Genesis 24:50–67 CEB)

Abraham did not choose a wife for his son directly, but he helped Isaac through his servant and his prayer because he understood the seriousness of the matter. Choosing a life partner is an extremely serious business if you wish your marriage to endure until death, as every believer should. Therefore, do not choose someone because he or she is wealthy, well connected, or physically attractive, or even because he or she is kind. Though such qualities may be worth noting to some extent, they remain minor considerations. The single most important characteristic of a potential spouse is his or her faith.

Amos 3:3 observes that two people cannot go in the same direction unless they agree. If you are a believer but choose an unbeliever simply because he or she is rich, good-looking, well educated, or fun at parties, then your life together will be built on a foundation doomed to crumble. Paul asked a series of pointed questions to this effect:

> Don't be tied up as equal partners with people who don't believe. What does righteousness share with that which is outside the Law? What relationship does light have with darkness? 15 What harmony does Christ have with Satan? What does a believer have in common with someone who doesn't believe? 16 What agreement can there be between God's temple and idols? Because we are the temple of the living God. Just as God said, I live with them, and I will move among them. I will be their God, and they will be my people. (2 Corinthians 6:14–16 CEB, emphasis in original)

Abraham warned his servant not to get Isaac a wife from among their neighbors because the other people of the land did not worship God or live in ways pleasing to Him (Genesis 24:3). Most people, now as then, don't think that beliefs are especially important in building a successful family, but Abraham knew better. However, since he had not been back to the land of his ancestors for more than forty years, he had no idea what relations of his might be living there. Abraham did not know of any specific woman who would make a good wife for Isaaac, but he had faith in God, and he had prayer; so he trained his servant how to pray.

You, too, can pray fervently, and God will bring you to exactly the right person at precisely the right time. Likewise, you should pray for your children in this regard, and you should teach your children to pray when they are ready to start a family of their own. If you truly believe in God and Jesus Christ, neither age nor circumstances nor anything else will discourage you from praying for your God-intended life partner.

Of course, a partnership is two-sided, and Rebekah was a willing partner to Isaac (Genesis 24:58). Marriage is a long journey, so preparation and cooperation are of vital importance. Unfortunately, many believers struggle in this; and the struggles are multiplied for spouses who do not share beliefs or have God present in their marriage. Remain patient and keep praying—remember, Isaac was already forty years old before he found Rebekah.

Now that Abraham had found a wife for his son, Isaac was content and prepared for life after his parents' deaths:

> Abraham took another wife, whose name was Keturah. She bore him Zimran, Jokshan, Medan, Midian, Ishbak and Shuah. ... 5 Abraham gave all he had to Isaac. 6 But to the sons of his concubines Abraham gave gifts, and while he was still living he sent them away from his son Isaac, eastward to the east country.
> 7 These are the days of the years of Abraham's life, 175 years. 8 Abraham breathed his last and died in a good old age, an old man and full of years, and was gathered to his people. 9 Isaac and Ishmael his sons buried him in the cave of Machpelah near Mamre, in the field of Ephron the son of Zohar the Hittite, 10 the field that Abraham had purchased from the Hittites. There Abraham was buried, with Sarah his wife. 11 After the death of Abraham, God blessed Isaac his son. And Isaac settled at Beer-lahai-roi. (Genesis 25:1, 5–11 ESV)

Abraham had married again after Sarah died, and he had more children. Some of his sons were not officially heirs because he did not marry their mothers as he had married Sarah and Keturah. Though that was the cultural practice at the time, Christians and other people today live under a rule of grace so that every child born outside of, or prior to, marriage is still rightly acknowledged and accepted.

THE CALL WITH PROMISE

Abraham started his journey to success at the age of seventy-five years and died a hundred years later. We will not reach Abraham's age, for God gradually limited the human lifespan to one hundred and twenty years (Genesis 6:3). Even so, you are not too old to start your own journey, and it is never too late to give your life to Christ.

Devoting your life completely to Christ is the best decision you will ever make. If you have already given your life to Him, rededicate and commit yourself fully to Him. Doing so ensures your success here on earth and also fulfilment in heaven.

CHAPTER FIFTEEN

THE PRINCIPLE OF ACCOUNTABILITY

Whatever we are doing here on earth will come to an end. We are all caretakers, and because of that, one day we will make an account to God. The word "accountability" means to be held liable, answerable, or responsible for what one has been given. Believers will be held accountable before the Lord someday for our actions, for what we did with what we have been given, and for what we didn't do that we should have done. Christian accountability is being able and ready to give an account for what we are up to. It is the realization that though we are already saved, we are nonetheless liable, responsible, and answerable to God, who "will test the quality of each person's work":

> "If anyone builds on this foundation using gold, silver, costly stones, wood, hay or straw, 13 their work will be shown for what it is, because the Day will bring it to light. It will be revealed with fire, and the fire will test the quality

of each person's work. 14 If what has been built survives, the builder will receive a reward. 15 If it is burned up, the builder will suffer loss but yet will be saved—even though only as one escaping through the flames. (1 Corinthians 3:12–15 NIV)

This verse should be a key scripture for every believer because although we are not saved by works, we will be rewarded according to what we did for Jesus Christ while on the earth. If our works were for our own glory and not for the glory of God, then our work is "burned" and we "will suffer loss" even though we "yet will be saved" in a narrow escape. However, if we do things for the glory of God alone, then we are building a more valuable and beautiful foundation and our works will endure the fire. If our good works are only for the purpose of being seen by others, and not of Christ, then they will burn up like "wood, hay or straw." In that case, we will have little or nothing to show for our life in our earthly bodies.

We also read about accountability in 2 Chronicles 19:6–7; Proverbs 11:14, 15:22, 24:6, and 27:17; Ezekiel 34:2–16 and 17–24; Matthew 12:36–37; and Galatians 6:1–10. As you read these scriptures, observe how accountability is especially vital for pastors and other spiritual leaders of God's flock.

Whether or not we are leaders in the church, for us to be able to make a proper account to God, we need to help each other. That is why we become accountable to one another. We do this by being open to what we are thinking and doing so we can receive encouragement, and reproof when needed. Accountability allows us to be answerable to one another, focusing on key relationships such as with our spouse, close friends, colleagues, coworkers, a boss, small group members, and our pastor. It is sharing, in confidence, our heartfelt Christian sojourn in an atmosphere of trust. Then we can give an answer for what we do; we can understand where we are weak and struggling and need help; we can reflect on where and how we are growing and what we are learning; and we can be encouraged.

We are accountable to God as well as to one another. We are declared clean before God by our Lord's work; however, we are still full of sin. We all have items and thoughts in our lives that diminish our relationship with God and our effectiveness with others. There is still a process on which to embark to become cleaner, and this is called sanctification. As Christians, we are in the process of practicing and growing in our faith, learning, and maturity all the days of our lives. If you really want to grow in faith and be effective in ministry, you must be held accountable; otherwise, you will fall, backslide, or be ineffective because of imbued pride.

Accountability is essential for every Christian to help reach his or her full potential; as noted above, it is an absolute mandate to those in leadership and ministry! Having other people around whom you can trust and get to know more deeply will enable you to know yourself-your strengths, weaknesses, and opportunities-more deeply. You will be able to see into your inner being and desires, as if into a mirror, and see if they line up to what God has planned for you. You will become more aware of your relationships, spiritual challenges, and blessings as your purpose and God's call unfold before you. Because you see life and God's Word more deeply, your behaviors and responses to others will change for the better

Accountability enables us to share our lives with one another in a deep, introspective way. This helps us to get to know ourselves and others in a deeper manner. Even though most of our relationships in life tend to be casual and superficial, we need deep connections; that is what God has made us for (Ecclesiastes 4:10–12).

In this, we can have a place to open up, share, and be challenged beyond sports, weather, fashion, or makeup. The goal is our spiritual formation, which is Christian maturity, growth, and character derived from God working in us and from us working out our faith with one another.

Accountability is not complaining about how life has dumped on us or an opportunity to put others down; rather, it is a "compact" (a deeper agreement beyond a contract) and system for the purpose of becoming more Christ-like (Psalm 133:1). A good accountability group will have questions, Bible study, prayer, listening, and support at its core.

Accountability is not about confrontation, either. We may, at times, need to be confronted and to confront another, but accountability is more about challenging one another to grow in Christ so there is no need to rebuke people. Accountability helps instill the warning precepts that God has given us, but it also involves the support, counsel, encouragement, and affirmation we all need.

Accountability enables us to be "one body in Christ, and individually we belong to each another" (Romans 12:5 CEB). This mutual belonging and connectedness enable us to lay aside the island mentality—we do not stand independent of one another. Because such interdependency exists within the Body of Christ, we are responsible to one another to do our part and to help others do theirs:

As it is, there are many parts, but one body. The eye cannot say to the hand, "I don't need you!" And the head cannot say to the feet, "I don't need you!" ... If one part suffers, every part suffers with it; if one part is honored, every part rejoices with it. (1 Corinthians 12:20–21, 26 CEB)

The key to effective accountability is to yield our pride to the necessity of being dependent on, and answerable to, one another. Our justification in Christ is no escape from bad things happening, because the world is still full of sin. In particular, leaders and pastors who are not accountable will be ineffective and then, eventually, will fall. God has called you to be the iron that sharpens others' iron, as their iron will sharpen you spiritually in return (Proverbs 27:17).

Accountability is a starting point for building and developing character, patience, and dependence on God's grace, as Abraham did by faith. We are accountable for our choices, and God approves when we are walking in Him. God does not approve when we are walking by ourselves, comfortable in our own petty presumptions, and ignoring His love and truth!

The Benefits of Accountability

Among the numerous benefits of practicing accountability is that it can help prevent burnout. Burnout occurs when our spiritual energies are totally exhausted and we have no will or vitality to make relationships, or to do whatever work we are supposed to do. We are completely worn out and spent. The stresses of life and the hassles of family will get us down and test our limits; even the best-run family will have this problem from time to time.

So, how can we tell whether we're simply tired or are experiencing burnout? First, we need to ask ourselves the accountability questions (see chapter 16). If we are operating in His precepts, it is probably just exhaustion. However, if we find ourselves being apathetic and detached from our families, we have a problem.

We must be on guard against the most destructive force—pride. Pride and arrogance will produce a superiority complex. We have to be willing to determine if we need an overhaul or just a good night's sleep. A mentor or accountability partner will help us see the warning signs.

Accountability can also help prevent stress. You can expect that people at home, church, and work, in addition to your loved ones, friends, acquaintances, and even pets will ask you for favors that require your time, resources, talents, or attention. This is good, and you should do what you can for others, but there will be times when they will deplete you, causing you stress. You cannot be everywhere, nor do everything!

Therefore, you must learn how to build a fence that says "I love you, but can you leave me alone for now!" The most important aspect to preventing stress is saying "no!" in a firm yet kind way, with an explanation of why. People deserve a reason, so don't just say "no!" Be honest, even if you just need time alone. Do not feel guilty; you have to take care of yourself first before you can care for others!

Be aware of stress that accompanies family outings and projects, especially during holidays. These occasions are stressful for many people, so take a look at why this is the case for you. Why does a particular situation, person, or possibility cause you stress? Is it fear?

To help prevent many of the stresses of life, learn to plan ahead. For big events, make sure you plan them out ahead of time and delegate. Remember, you are not indispensable; if you think you are, you need help from a good counselor or

THE PRINCIPLE OF ACCOUNTABILITY

pastor! Do not try to do too many things or take on too many projects, especially if they are new to you. In particular, do not allow people to force responsibilities on you just because you have shouldered them before. They need to respect you and your time.

Accountability helps make us aware of intrusions and stress. It may take others to notice and tell us to take breaks from other people so we can have more time with family and God. Accountably will help refocus our spiritual awareness and replenish our physical energy.

Furthermore, accountability helps us be aware of bad habits, anxieties, phobias, and mental disorders that contribute to stress; those can keep us from our relationships and functions with family and church.If you are a procrastinator, then force yourself to begin early. Once you figure out that life is easier and less stressful when you do things on the early side, you will make it a habit of it. Just make sure you seek help from a good counselor or trained pastor with serious disorders.

Accountability is often associated with seeking help for a problem or addiction, such as drinking, drugs, smoking, or pornography. However, the emphasis should be on spiritual growth, which infuses our thinking and behaviors and helps in overcoming addictions. Yet it's about more than overcoming addictions; it is about being overcome with Christ as Lord of our lives!

Effective accountability emphasizes the building of deep, quality relationships that will help us with the following aspects of our spiritual development:

- Adhering to God's Word and call
- Learning to commune with God more deeply so we can respond to His precepts more rapidly and thoroughly
- Prayer that is not just about our personal needs but also about the needs of others
- Reigniting our passion for Christ
- Becoming teachable, and examining our thinking and behaviors
- Being willing to recognize sin in our lives and in the lives of others, too
- Being willing to learn about ourselves
- Being willing to have healing in our lives
- Being willing to see the needs of others
- Being willing to overcome, and being on guard concerning weaknesses and strengths
- Being able to trust, share, and commune with another person in depth
- Being willing to overcome issues that are bad for us
- Knowing that we need others to keep us on track
- Being willing to be challenged, convicted, molded, and sharpened so we can change and grow
- Developing better and deeper fellowship and unity with others
- Establishing a platform for being transformed and renewed in Christ
- Becoming more sensitive and discerning
- Learning to develop the fruit of the Spirit and exercise it
- Being willing to confess and hear others in love and confidentiality-without judgment
- Being encouraged and encouraging others
- Developing godly, Christ-like character
- Learning to take risks, be vulnerable, and overcome rejection and betrayal

- Learning that God has called us to be involved in the lives of others and that we are not to be lone ranger Christians
- Learning that we are to be patient, because accountability is built over time
- Learning that deep connections do not just happen on their own between church services; we have to work at them in community
- Learning that we are at our best when we are being real and authentic
- Learning about Christ's redemption and our ability to change
- Learning we can be used by God to serve as change agents in the lives of others
- Learning that relationships require effort and commitment
- Developing harmony with others so we can communicate, and being transparent without being defensive
- Developing maturity and spiritual growth
- Leaning to be humble and wise
- Allowing the work of the Holy Spirit within us and being used by Him in the lives of others as well
- Developing the ability to break through the noise of our will and desires, as we need a godly perspective we can hear over that noise
- Remembering that God is in control, even in times of dire stress and confusion
- Trusting in God and keeping His standards because they are best for us; there is no better way than His Way!
- Knowing we need accountability for our faith development, support, and growth
- Knowing that accountability takes our initiative, commitment, and persistence
- Realizing we have no need to hide our sins from those who are entrusted to help us deal with them

THE CALL WITH PROMISE

See also 1 Thessalonians, 5:14 Colossians, and 3:16 Hebrews 3:13.

Becoming Accountable

God designed the church as the Body of Christ. Thus, we are called to unity and cooperation so we can be there for one another in times of joy and happiness as well as stress. We are called to encourage and equip as well as to hold each other responsible to the commitment we have made in Christ as Lord.

To get involved in an accountability group, first look for an existing one you can join, such as a small group through your church—or a neighboring church if your church does not have one. Make sure it is gender-specific, having either men only or women only. Most of these groups are found under men's or women's ministries. If none is available or you are not led to one, hook up with another two or three people and start your own. You can find people through a church leader or pastor.

During this process, make sure you are in prayer, asking God to lead you in the right direction. The substance of why and what you are doing is more important than the form of how you do it. The key to making this work is for you and the other participants to be open, submissive, listening, and authentic so you can confess your sins in a safe, confidential environment.

What a Good Accountability Program/Partner Will Have

- Look for confidentiality as paramount.
- Look for people whom you already know or have a connection with, such as a common interest or season in life.

THE PRINCIPLE OF ACCOUNTABILITY

- Look for people whom you respect and trust, who are mature in their faith and character, and from whom you can learn so you can develop closeness and share shortcomings.
- Look for people who maintain a loving and respectful attitude.
- Make sure you use God's Word; it is your standard for faith and practice.
- Make sure no one dominates unless it is a teacher teaching. Have equal airtime so all can be involved. If you are in a larger group, have a teaching time, then break down into sub-groups for accountability questions and prayer.
- Be willing to be flexible and surrender your time when another person needs extra time and care.
- Participants need to respect the feelings and time of others, and to speak the truth in love.
- Communicate ground rules or a code of conduct, clearly emphasizing confidentiality and equal time.
- Make sure prayer is the focus.
- Seek guidance from others who can shepherd you, who have "been there, done that" — who have weathered the storms and are able to share it. Look for people you can shepherd and guide faithfully.
- Seek those who can help you adhere to God's standards rather than to the world's standards.
- Seek faithfulness and constancy.
- Use humor, but not at the expense of others.
- Be committed and encourage others to be so, too..
- Remember, the primary purpose is to get yourself aligned with God's love, call, and precepts over all else.
- Be aware of your pride, and never allow your maturity and growth to be a source of pride or use it to put others down.

- What you do not want is to be disciplined by people who are prideful, who only care about themselves, or who are irritable, presumptive, "too busy," and neglectful of others! Make sure you are not this way to others!

There is no best way or program to "do" accountability. It can be a "one-on-one" mentorship or a large group that is subdivided into smaller ones; it can meet for one hour or two, once a week or every other week. The important thing is to do it, remain committed, and follow Christ rather than yourself. If you do not "click" with the people in your group or feel you do not have a certain level of trust, that is okay; this may not be the group or person for you. Look for another person or start another group.

How can we do this? By seeing others with the eyes of Christ—to see love, compassion, and forgiveness. Take the "one another passages" to heart when you instruct, warn, or even chastise; do it in the parameters of the fruit of the Spirit, without judgment or commendation. When we rely on God and build one another up, we grow in faith and maturity and become more effective to one another. This is reciprocal, and will replicate and continue.

So, what is the final obstacle remaining? The commitment to make it continual. Accountability is not just for a time; it is for all times, and requires our discipline and dedication to keep at it. If we stop, we soon go back to our fears and complacency. When this happens, sin that before was of no consequence has now grown big and is knocking on your door. Commitment is essential to the successful functioning of anything precious, from a friendship to marriage to being a member of a church. We must be committed and continual. Commitment brings about hope and growth through sacrifice as we pour ourselves into it while being fueled by our Lord.

Take it slow and easy. Don't try, or even expect, to delve immediately into the deepest, darkest corners of your life. Begin by having your close friends hold you accountable for things like regular prayer and integrity issues. As you see the results and benefits of this, you will also be building up trust, which is necessary for accountability in more personal and private areas. If you need further help in this area, seek a qualified and trusted pastor or Christian counselor. Above all, seek someone to whom you can be accountable. Do not merely trust yourself; have a small group or mentor ask you these questions on a regular basis!

Remember that Christian maturity and character is "Christ-likeness," becoming more like our Lord by living out His precepts. This is not a destination until we are called home to eternity. Meanwhile, we who are on this journey must make the most our opportunities. As Peter wrote:

The end of all things is near. Therefore be alert and of sober mind so that you may pray. 8 Above all, love each other deeply, because love covers over a multitude of sins. 9 Offer hospitality to one another without grumbling. 10 Each of you should use whatever gift you have received to serve others, as faithful stewards of God's grace in its various forms. 11 If anyone speaks, they should do so as one who speaks the very words of God. If anyone serves, they should do so with the strength God provides, so that in all things God may be praised through Jesus Christ. To him be the glory and the power for ever and ever. Amen. (1 Peter 4:7–11 NIV)

CHAPTER SIXTEEN

ACCOUNTABILITY QUESTIONS

"Therefore confess your sins to each other and pray for each other so that you may be healed. The prayer of a righteous man is powerful and effective." (James 5:16 NIV)

Accountability allows us to be answerable to one another as we focus on improving our key relationships—with people such as our spouse, close friends, colleagues, coworkers, a boss, small group members, or a pastor. Accountability will also enhance our integrity, maturity, character relationships in general, and our growth in Christ. Accountability is sharing, in confidence, our heartfelt Christian sojourn in an atmosphere of trust so we can give an answer for what we do, see where we need help, understand our struggles and where we are weak, and be encouraged to stay on track, seek prayer, care, and support when we fail, and model guideposts for one another to keep us going.

QUESTIONS

Below are some key accountability questions you can ask yourself and/or have a mentor ask you.

1. Have you been spending significant time with God through His Word, prayer, quiet time, devotions, and other spiritual disciplines? How much? How constantly? Is He your driving force?
2. What blocks your growth in Christ? What blocks you from growing more mature and effectual in your other relationships?
3. How has your time with God been? Have you been praying for others? Are you satisfied with the time you spent with our Lord this week? How so? What can you do to improve it?
4. Have you faithfully served the Lord, His people, and the lost?
5. Did you go and participate in church activities and worship this week? How so? Why not?
6. Did you set spiritual goals this week? What were they? Did you achieve your spiritual goals?
7. Have you made your family a priority? What noteworthy activity or deed did you do for your spouse and/or family?
8. How have you struggled with sin? What are the sins that have weighed down your walk with God this week?
9. What did you do to enhance your relationship with your spouse/friends? What can you do to make that relationship better?
10. In what ways has God blessed you this week? How have you shared your blessings?
11. What disappointments did you face? Did they consume your thoughts? What did you do about it? What can you learn?

12. Have you filled the mandates of your calling, work, and education, practicing excellence and giving one hundred percent for His glory?
13. Have you committed any sexual sin? Did you look at someone lustfully? Have you been alone in a compromising situation? Have you been flirtatious? Have you struggled with pornography or "romance novels"? Have you exposed yourself to any sexually oriented material? Did you put yourself in a situation with a member of the opposite sex that could appear to be compromising, even though it may not have been?
14. Have you shared your faith? In what ways? How can you improve? Have you had an opportunity to share with a non-Christian?
15. How well are you handling your finances right now? Have your financial dealings been questionable?
16. Have you been trustworthy? Have you lied? Stolen? Cheated? Been dishonest or manipulative? Have you elevated yourself over another for your own personal agenda? Have you practiced integrity in your language and attitude?
17. Have you allowed the media and its distortions in TV, music, and movies to influence you unduly? Have you given ground to spiritually unhealthy peer pressure?
18. Have you been prideful? Have you been guilty of gossip or anger? Have you slandered others and failed to control your tongue? Have you been greedy or shown indifference toward others? These types of behaviors most hinder people from knowing and trusting Christ!
19. Have you demonstrated a servant's heart? How so? What have you done for someone else this week?
20. Did you struggle with a disappointment this week? How did you handle it?

21. Have you respected and treated your classmates, co-workers, and peers graciously by showing them compassion and the love of God in your words and deeds? What can you do to enhance your relationships in school or the workplace?
22. How would you assess your characters, judging on the basis of Galatians 5:22–23 versus Galatians 5:19–21?
23. How did you practice joy this week? Have you had a thankful attitude toward God? Have you struggled with anger toward God? How so? What can you do about it?
24. Have you taken care of the temple of the Holy Spirit with rest, sleep, exercise, balanced eating, and other healthy habits? Have you engaged in addictions, gluttony, or substance abuse?
25. Have you kept your thoughts pure?
26. Are you giving to the Lord's work with your time, talent, and treasures? What about financially?
27. What do you need to do to improve your relationships with God and with others?
28. What do you see as your number one need or struggle for this next week?
29. Have you been less than wholly truthful in your responses to the above questions?
30. How can your spouse, pastor, family members, support group, or other accountability partner help you to grow more accountable?

Take it slow and easy. Don't try, or even expect, to delve immediately into the deepest, darkest corners of your life. Begin by having your close friends hold you accountable for things like praying regularly and integrity issues. As you see the benefit and results of this, you will also be building up trust, which is necessary for accountability in more personal and private areas.

THE CALL WITH PROMISE

If you need further help in this area, seek a qualified and trusted pastor or Christian counselor. Also, seek someone to whom you can be accountable. Do not just trust yourself; have a small group or mentor ask you these questions on a regular basis!

If you fall away from these questions, or refuse to have someone hold you to them, then Satan will have a foothold in your life. These questions are not just for the pastor or church leader; they are for all Christians who want to live a life of integrity and significance. The failure to have accountability will produce sin. At that point, it is not a question of if you may fall, but rather when you will engage in sin and destroy everything in your life. The relationships and ministry God has given you as well as your family and those around you, for generations to come, will be destroyed. Yes, there can be restitution and restoration, but the cost can never be completely repaid.

Every Christian should consider having an accountability partner with whom he or she can pray, talk, confide, and confess. An accountability partner can be there to encourage you, rebuke you, teach you, rejoice with you, and weep with you. Accountability is a critical aspect of your battle to overcome sin and secure success in every aspect of your life!

CONCLUSION

Abraham did not believe in religion or denomination; he believed in God. Religion and denomination are killing us softly. Believers have placed so much of their faith in rituals and doctrines that their relationships with Jesus Christ are suffering. Of those who spread beliefs contrary to His message and example, Jesus warned us:

"Watch out for false prophets. They come to you in sheep's clothing, but inwardly they are ferocious wolves. 16 By their fruit you will recognize them. Do people pick grapes from thornbushes, or figs from thistles? 17 Likewise, every good tree bears good fruit, but a bad tree bears bad fruit. ...

21 "Not everyone who says to me, 'Lord, Lord,' will enter the kingdom of heaven, but only the one who does the will of my Father who is in heaven. 22 Many will say to me on that day, 'Lord, Lord, did we not prophesy in your name and in your name drive out demons and in your name perform many miracles?' 23 Then I will tell them plainly, 'I never knew you. Away from me, you evildoers!'

24 "Therefore everyone who hears these words of mine and puts them into practice is like a wise man who built his house on the rock. 25 The rain came down, the streams rose, and the winds blew and beat against that house; yet it did not fall, because it had its foundation on the rock. 26 But everyone who hears these words of mine and does not put them into practice is like a foolish man who built his house on sand. 27 The rain came down, the streams rose, and the winds blew

and beat against that house, and it fell with a great crash." (Matthew 7:15–17, 21–27 NIV)

We have one true God, who can help us succeed in all things when we believe in Him. No doubt, in some or all respects, you have been trying to handle life yourself; but God teaches us to "call upon me in the day of trouble; I will deliver you, and you shall glorify me" (Psalm 50:15 ESV). He says also, "Call to me and I will answer you, and will tell you great and hidden things that you have not known" (Jeremiah 33:3 ESV).

Remember the following names of God and notice how they are used in the Bible. Try to use them in your prayers.

EL-GIBHOR: "Mighty God"

For to us a child is born, to us a son is given; and the government shall be upon his shoulder, and his name shall be called Wonderful Counselor, Mighty God, Everlasting Father, Prince of Peace. (Isaiah 9:6 ESV)

EL-OLAM: "Everlasting God"

Lord, you have been our dwelling place
in all generations.
2 Before the mountains were brought forth,
or ever you had formed the earth and the world,
from everlasting to everlasting you are God.
3 You return man to dust
and say, "Return, O children of man! (Psalm 90:1–3 ESV)

JEHOVAH-SHAMMAH: "The LORD Is There"

"The circumference of the city shall be 18,000 cubits. And the name of the city from that time on shall be, The LORD Is There." (Ezekiel 48:35 ESV)

ELOHIM: "God Creator, Mighty and Strong"
In the beginning, God created the heavens and the earth. (Genesis 1:1 ESV)

EL SHADDAI: "God Almighty"
...how he swore to the LORD and vowed to the Mighty One of Jacob... (Psalm 132:2 ESV)

...yet his bow remained unmoved;
his arms were made agile
by the hands of the Mighty One of Jacob
(from there is the Shepherd, the Stone of Israel)... (Genesis 49:24 ESV)

ADONAI: "LORD"
But Abram said, "Sovereign LORD, what can you give me since I remain childless and the one who will inherit my estate is Eliezer of Damascus?" (Genesis 15:2 NIV)

JEHOVAH-JIREH: "The LORD Will Provide"
So Abraham called the name of that place, "The LORD will provide"; as it is said to this day, "On the mount of the LORD it shall be provided." (Genesis 22:14 ESV)

JEHOVAH-RAPHA: "The LORD Who Heals"
..."If you will diligently listen to the voice of the LORD your God, and do that which is right in his eyes, and give ear to his commandments and keep all his statutes, I put none of the diseases on you that I put on the Egyptians, for I am the LORD, your healer." (Exodus 15:26 ESV)

JEHOVAH-NISSI: "The LORD Our Banner"
And Moses built an altar and called the name of it, The LORD Is My Banner... (Exodus 17:15 ESV)

JEHOVAH-M'KADDESH: "The LORD Who Makes Holy"

"Keep my decrees and follow them. I am the LORD, who makes you holy." (Leviticus 20:8 NIV)

JEHOVAH-SHALOM: "The LORD Our Peace"

Then Gideon built an altar there to the LORD and called it, The LORD Is Peace. To this day it still stands at Ophrah, which belongs to the Abiezrites. (Judges 6:24 ESV)

JEHOVAH-ELOHIM: "LORD God"

These are the generations
of the heavens and the earth when they were created,
in the day that the LORD God made the earth and the heavens. (Genesis 2:4 ESV)

JEHOVAH-TSIDKENU: "The LORD Our Righteousness"

"In those days Judah will be saved, and Jerusalem will dwell securely. And this is the name by which it will be called: 'The LORD is our righteousness.'" (Jeremiah 33:16 ESV)

JEHOVAH-ROHI: "The LORD Our Shepherd"

The LORD is my shepherd, I shall not want. (Psalm 23:1 ESV)

My final advice to you comes from the book of James:

> Know this, my beloved brothers: let every person be quick to hear, slow to speak, slow to anger; 20 for the anger of man does not produce the righteousness of God. 21 Therefore put away all filthiness and rampant wickedness and receive with meekness the implanted word, which is able to save your souls.
> 22 But be doers of the word, and not hearers only, deceiving yourselves. 23 For if anyone is a hearer of the word and not

a doer, he is like a man who looks intently at his natural face in a mirror. 24 For he looks at himself and goes away and at once forgets what he was like. 25 But the one who looks into the perfect law, the law of liberty, and perseveres, being no hearer who forgets but a doer who acts, he will be blessed in his doing.

26 If anyone thinks he is religious and does not bridle his tongue but deceives his heart, this person's religion is worthless. 27 Religion that is pure and undefiled before God, the Father, is this: to visit orphans and widows in their affliction, and to keep oneself unstained from the world. (James 1:19–27 ESV)

May God bless you!

ABOUT THE AUTHOR

Richmond Donkor is Author, songwriter, singer, self-development coach, Evangelist, Pastor, teacher, motivational speaker and philanthropist. He is the author of 3 steps to Overcome Poverty, The Call With Promise; From wretch to Riches, How to Evangelize With Confidence, The Ultimate Wife, The Ultimate Husband, The Ultimate Dream Family and Created to Lead. Richmond has been preaching, teaching, training, and planting churches in South-East Asia and currently he is the associate pastor at the Restored House Chapel Ministries in Vancouver, Canada. He enjoys reading, writing, praying, and singing praises and worship songs.

Learn more about him from his website:

http://www.evangelistrichmond.com.

Made in the USA
San Bernardino, CA
07 February 2018